SPECIAL CAMPAIGN SERIES. No. 5

THE WATERLOO CAMPAIGN

SPECIAL CAMPAIGN SERIES.   No. 5

THE WATERLOO CAMPAIGN

A Study

By
LIEUT.-COL. SISSON C. PRATT
Late R.A.
Author of "Saarbrück to Paris," etc.

WITH SEVEN MAPS AND SKETCHES

" Gude gear gangs in little bouk."—*Scotch Proverb*

The Naval & Military Press Ltd

Published by

The Naval & Military Press Ltd
Unit 5 Riverside, Brambleside
Bellbrook Industrial Estate
Uckfield, East Sussex
TN22 1QQ England

Tel: +44 (0)1825 749494

www.naval-military-press.com
www.nmarchive.com

Cover illustration:
The Storming of Plancenoit by Ludwig Elsholtz

In reprinting in facsimile from the original, any imperfections are inevitably reproduced and the quality may fall short of modern type and cartographic standards.

Print and page size has been increased over the original publications to accommodate the oversized maps.

PREFACE

THE centenary of the Wars of Liberation is now close at hand, and from the hitherto unpublished archives and private records that are known to exist in Germany some fresh light will probably soon be thrown on the downfall of Napoleon. This brief study of a notable campaign may be of some help to the student of the past and the historian of the future.

I append a list of the principal works consulted.

H.	. .	H. Houssaye. 1815. *Waterloo.* 55th Ed. 1906.
R.	. .	J. C. Ropes. *The Campaign of Waterloo.* 4th Ed. 1906.
G.	. .	Colonel A. Grouard. *La Critique de la Campagne de* 1815. 1904.
		Colonel A. Grouard. *Reponse a M. Houssaye.* 1906.
L. V.	. .	Major-General von Lettow Vorbeck. *Napoleon's Untergang.* 1906.
De Bas	.	Colonel F. de Bas. *Prins Frederik der Niederlanden.* 3rd vol. 1904.
Hart.	. .	J. von Pflugk - Harttung. *Vorgeschichte der Schlacht bei Belle Alliance.* 1903.
		J. von Pflugk-Harttung. *Das 1 Preussiche Korps bei Belle Alliance.* 1905.
Pol.	. .	Generale A. Pollio. *Waterloo (1815) con nuovi documenti.* 1906.

Though the above books embody the researches of all well-known authorities of the past century, I have had occasion to refer directly to Sibborne, Charras, Chesney, and others. I am also indebted to the works of Sir Herbert Maxwell, J. Holland Rose, Oman, and some less known English writers. In all cases I have made a suitable acknowledgment. The student who looks out the references will be able to acquaint himself with many details which are necessarily omitted from this designedly brief narrative.

CONTENTS

CHAP.		PAGE
I.	THE GENERAL SITUATION.	3
II.	PLAN OF CAMPAIGN	13
III.	THE CONTENDING ARMIES	23
IV.	THE PASSAGE OF THE SAMBRE	33
V.	BLÜCHER AND WELLINGTON— JUNE 15	49
VI.	THE MORNING OF JUNE 16. THE FRENCH ARMY	61
VII.	THE MORNING OF JUNE 16. THE ALLIED ARMIES	73
VIII.	THE BATTLE OF QUATRE-BRAS	81
IX.	THE BATTLE OF LIGNY	95
X.	THE D'ERLON EPISODE	109
XI.	THE MORNING OF JUNE 17. NAPOLEON	119
XII.	THE ENGLISH RETREAT	125
XIII.	THE PRUSSIAN RETREAT	135
XIV.	THE PURSUIT BY GROUCHY	145
XV.	THE BATTLE OF WATERLOO	157
XVI.	THE COMBAT AT WAVRE	187
XVII.	THE RETREAT OF GROUCHY	195

LIST OF MAPS AND PLANS

1. POSITION OF ALLIED FORCES ON JUNE 14.
2. MILITARY OPERATIONS, JUNE 15–20.
3. MAPS OF FERRARIS USED BY NAPOLEON.
4. THE BATTLE OF WATERLOO.
5. THE PASSAGE OF THE SAMBRE.
6. THE BATTLE OF QUATRE-BRAS.
7. THE BATTLE OF LIGNY.

APPENDIX

		PAGE
1.	NAPOLEON TO NEY. EXTRACT FROM LETTER DATED CHARLEROI, JUNE 16, 8 A.M.	203
2.	SOULT TO NEY. EXTRACT FROM ORDER DATED CHARLEROI, JUNE 16, 7 A.M.	203
3.	SOULT TO NEY. EXTRACT FROM ORDER DATED CHARLEROI, JUNE 16, 10 A.M.	204
4.	SOULT TO NEY. EXTRACT FROM ORDER DATED FLEURUS, JUNE 16, 2 P.M.	204
5.	SOULT TO NEY. EXTRACT FROM ORDER DATED FLEURUS, JUNE 16, 3.15 P.M.	205
6.	NEY TO SOULT. LETTER RECENTLY DISCOVERED DATED FRASNES, JUNE 16, 10 P.M.	205
7.	NAPOLEON TO GROUCHY. EXTRACT FROM LETTER DATED CHARLEROI, JUNE 16, 8 A.M	206
8.	WELLINGTON TO BLÜCHER. LETTER DATED HEIGHTS BEHIND FRASNES, JUNE 16, 10.30 A.M.	207
9.	SOULT TO NEY. EXTRACT FROM LETTER DATED FLEURUS, JUNE 17, 8 A.M.	207
10.	SOULT TO NEY. ORDER DATED LIGNY, JUNE 17, 12 NOON	208
11.	BERTRAND TO GROUCHY. EXTRACT FROM LETTER DATED LIGNY, JUNE 17, 11.45 A.M.	208
12.	GROUCHY TO NAPOLEON. EXTRACT FROM LETTER DATED GEMBLOUX, JUNE 17, 10 P.M.	208
13.	GROUCHY TO NAPOLEON. EXTRACT FROM LETTER DATED WALHAIN, JUNE 18, 11 A.M.	209
14.	SOULT TO GROUCHY. EXTRACT FROM LETTER DATED LE CAILLOU, JUNE 18, 10 A.M.	210
15.	SOULT TO GROUCHY. EXTRACT FROM LETTER DATED JUNE 18, 1 P.M.	210
16.	D'ERLON TO PRINCE OF MOSCOW. EXTRACT FROM LETTER DATED PARIS, 1829	211
17.	CHASSÉ TO LORD HILL. EXTRACT FROM LETTER DATED BOURGET, JULY 5, 1815	212
18.	ORDER OF BATTLE OF ANGLO-ALLIED ARMY	212
19.	DISTRIBUTION OF ALLIED FORCE AT WATERLOO	214
20.	NOTE ON STRENGTH OF THE ARMIES	216
21.	THE ATTACK OF ZIETEN AND ITS CONSEQUENCES	217

THE GENERAL SITUATION

CHAPTER I

THE GENERAL SITUATION

The General Situation—The Allied Armies—The Plan of Operations—The Armies of France—The Military Policy of Napoleon.

THE occupation of Paris by the Allies in 1814 led to the deposition of Napoleon and his removal to Elba as a state prisoner. The monarchy, restored by foreign bayonets, was welcomed in Paris, and, despite rumours of discontent in the provinces, the authority of the Bourbon king was nowhere challenged. The summer of 1814 opened in hope, but closed in despair. To reorganize the finances of the kingdom, effect a settlement of the land question, and satisfy the exorbitant demands of the *émigrés* and the Church were matters of no little difficulty. The Bourbon régime was quite incapable of dealing with the situation, and one unpopular measure after another undermined the stability of the government. Towards the close of the year the country seethed with discontent, and the disbanded soldiery of the empire became a serious menace to good order.

Meanwhile, the Allied troops, still at war strength, were marching to their homes, and the representatives of the Great Powers assembled at Vienna to divide the spoils of conquest.

The antagonism of France to the Bourbon dynasty, the disorders in the provinces, the discontent in the army, and the quarrels of the coalition, did not escape the notice of the astute exile of Elba. At the first favourable opportunity he evaded his gaolers, and with a few of his bodyguard and personal adherents landed in France on March 1, 1815. His dramatic and triumphal march on Paris has often been described; and on March 20 he re-entered the Tuileries, and assumed again the reins of government.

The empire, thus easily restored in France, had now to encounter the wrath of a united Europe. The work of 1814 had to be done again, and the Allied Sovereigns, in view of a common danger, made a fresh coalition, and appeal to the sword. Austria, Prussia, Russia and England, with 150,000 men each, were at once to take the field and remain under arms " till Bonaparte should have been rendered absolutely incapable of stirring up further trouble"; while England, besides granting large subsidies, was to make up in money any deficiency of men. It was war to the knife, and the numerous armies put in motion were all animated by a fierce determination to annihilate the common foe.

The Allied Armies
The troops of Prussia, Austria and the smaller German States were spread over a wide tract of country, from the Oder to the Danube, while the leading Russian corps had reached the Vistula. A mixed force of Prussians, Anglo-Hanoverians, Dutch and Belgians were extended in cantonments on the northern frontier, between the Rhine and the Scheldt, while the Austrians and Piedmontese in considerable numbers were in Italy. The troops at the disposal of the coalition were, numerically, more powerful than any army that could be raised in France.

But to concentrate the dispersed forces, and make them act in unison, required time, and a well-considered strategical plan.

The Plan of Operations
It was obvious that the superior numbers of the Allies would enable a converging advance to be made on Paris from the north and the east. Several schemes were under consideration. Both Wellington and Blücher were anxious that hostilities should begin without waiting for the arrival of the Russians or other distant troops. It was pointed out that the power of Napoleon was daily increasing, and that prompt action would be seconded by the Royalist operations in La Vendée. The council held at Vienna under the presidency of the Czar was, however, loth to take any risks, and finally adopted the plan of Schwartzenberg, the execution of which was delayed until the last days of June.

H. 94
The forces available were estimated to be of the following strength :—

The Netherlands Army (Wellington)	93,000
The Prussian Army (Blücher)	117,000
The Army of the Rhine (Schwartzenberg)	210,000
The Russian Army (Barclay de Tolly)	150,000
The Army of Italy (Frimont)	50,000
The Army of Naples (Bianchi)	25,000

The six armies 645,000 strong were to cross the frontier simultaneously, and the four principal armies were to make a concentric movement on Paris. Wellington passing between Maubeuge and Beaumont was to advance by way of Peronne; while Blücher, crossing between Phillippeville and Givet, moved by Laon. The Army of the Rhine, from Basle and Sarreguemines, was to take the Langres road, while the Russians from Saarlouis and Saarbrück adopted the Nancy route. On the left the army of Italy was to advance on Lyons, while the Austrian troops from Naples made their way to Provence.

The Armies of France On his return from Elba, Napoleon found that the military forces of the country had been reduced to some 210,000 men, of whom but a fraction were in a condition to take the field. An attack from the forces of the coalition was imminent, and no time had to be lost in raising the strength of the army, and placing the threatened frontiers in a state of defence.

Within a week after his entry into Paris the Emperor, without waiting for mobilization to commence, decreed the formation in eight army corps of the troops near Paris, the garrisons of the frontier towns, and the various regiments in the provinces that had flocked to his standard. By incorporating the men absent on leave, recalling to the colours the many deserters, and appealing for volunteers, a large increase was at once made in the field army. The mobilization of the National Guard, and the utilization of men on the lists of the navy, gendarmerie, customs officials, etc., swelled the total numbers that in one way or another would be available for service. Third battalions to each regiment were rapidly formed, the depôts were filled with partially trained men, while the places of the regular troops in the fortresses were gradually taken by the mobilized National Guards.

H. 36 About the end of May the active army had been raised to a strength of 291,000 men, while behind them, in second line, was an auxiliary force some 222,000 strong.

The distribution of the active French forces at this period was briefly as follows :—

The Army of the North (Napoleon)	124,139
The Army of the Rhine (Rapp)	19,992
The Army of the Alps (Suchet)	17,317
The Army of the Pyrenees	7,820
The Army of the West	10,000
Var and Jura Corps	8,864
In Depôts	65,118
On the Way to Join	13,934
Fortress Artillery	11,233
In Hospital	8,162
In Elba and Abroad	4,700
Total	291,279 men[1]

War material for this large force had, to a great extent, to be created. The government of the Restoration had neglected to replenish the stores, exhausted by the campaigns of past years. The artillery had a fair complement of guns, but horses, harness and ammunition were woefully deficient. Muskets and cartridges were scarce, and a large number of horses were required to mount the cavalry.

The arsenals, factories and workshops throughout France were worked to their utmost limits; the Departments were put under requisition to provide horses, and, by dint of a large expenditure both at home and abroad, it at last became possible to put the field army on an effective footing.

It was necessary, moreover, to place the frontier

[1] An analysis of the above figures shows that at the beginning of June the field armies in France had a strength of about 190,000 men. With the exception of the Army of the North, the troops were badly off as to equipment.

fortresses in a good state of defence, and to convert both Lyons and Paris into strong, entrenched camps. To repair and strengthen existing works, to obtain a sufficient supply of cannon and ammunition, and to properly garrison and provision the defences of the country, required both time and money.

H 26   By the middle of June the fortified places of the first rank were supplied for four months, while the convoys of the Army of the North carried reserve provisions for a week. Every day showed an increase in the military power of France, and the best policy to adopt was a matter for serious consideration.

Military Policy of Napoleon   Napoleon, by his spies, was kept well acquainted with the projects of the Allied Sovereigns. It was evident, in June, that the blow was about to fall, and the manner in which it could be best met has been discussed at length in the *Memoirs*. With a strong line of frontier defences, a capital in process of being fortified, and an army that only required time to develop its full strength, it was obvious that great value might be attached to a defensive policy.

Assuming that the frontier was crossed at the end of June, it would take the Allies nearly a month to advance from the Rhine to Paris. The armies of Italy would be for some time kept in check by the combined forces of Suchet and Rapp. For guarding the lines of communication, and masking the frontier fortresses on the main lines of invasion, at least 150,000 men would be required. The total numbers of the armies of the coalition, on their arrival between the Oise and the Seine, would not exceed 420,000 men, and to these the

Emperor would be able to oppose a highly trained force of old soldiers, some 200,000 strong, whose operations would be based on an entrenched camp defended by 80,000 men. Were a defensive attitude to be taken up, the composite nature of the Allied forces, and the divergent views of their commanders, might possibly enable Napoleon to repeat with success his exploits of 1814.

To the student of strategy the thought will naturally arise as to whether the numerical strength of the French forces would not militate against movements the success of which depended on rapid marching and the element of surprise. The Emperor himself took a hopeful view of the situation, and his views are supported by the great authority of Jomini and Clausewitz.

But the purely military considerations were dominated by the politics of the day. Though chief of the army, Napoleon was but insecurely seated on his throne. Disaffection was widely spread through the provinces, and a policy that surrendered a third of France without resistance would be most unpopular to a nation that had already been bereft of most of its conquests. The population was weary of war, and would only support a leader who gave some immediate and decisive proof of his powers. Further delay was impossible, and the alternative policy was to assume the offensive in the only quarter that afforded a prospect of success.

The Anglo-Dutch and Prussian armies were known to lie in widely extended cantonments in Belgium, and it appeared feasible that they might be surprised and defeated in detail.

Time would not admit of the recall of the troops from the eastern frontier, but the

Army of the North, 124,000 strong, could easily be concentrated for an immediate advance.

A great victory would cause Belgium to rally to the French flag, increase the disaffection known to exist among some of the German auxiliaries, and possibly lead to the advent of a peace ministry in England. With the éclat of success, a reinforced army, and the assistance of Rapp, the Austrian and Russian forces could be afterwards dealt with. A visionary scheme perhaps, but every world maker is visionary. Its success was possible, nay, even probable, and that it resulted in disaster was due to a series of errors and misunderstandings of great historical interest.

THE PLAN OF CAMPAIGN

CHAPTER II

PLAN OF CAMPAIGN

Allied Position in Belgium—The Routes of Invasion—The Plan of Campaign—The Concentration on Beaumont—The Orders of the 14th of June for Advance—The Attitude of the Allied Commanders—Views of Napoleon.

Allied Position in Belgium THE Anglo-Dutch and Prussian armies—some 220,000 strong—were, for convenience of supply, distributed in cantonments that covered a front of 100 miles from Liège to Tournai, and stretched back to 40 miles from the frontier. The army of Wellington was dependent for its munitions of war on Ostend and Antwerp, while that of Blücher was based on Cologne and the Rhine. On the approach of an enemy the Allied armies would necessarily concentrate and then endeavour to unite.

To fall on each army in detail necessitated a veiled concentration on the frontier, followed by an advance which should be on the nature of a surprise.

Routes of Invasion An attack on the outer flank of either Wellington or Blücher presented no special advantages, and involved the certainty that the major portion of the force, whose communications were threatened, would fall back on its ally. The lines of advance were practically restricted to the three main roads, leading from the frontier to Brussels by way of Tournai, Mons and Charleroi. The dismantled fortifications of the two former towns had been put in a position to offer some resistance, and they would have either to be attacked or masked. Neither time nor troops could be afforded for such operations, and the utilization of these routes would lead the French army into the centre of the Anglo-Dutch cantonments. Between Charleroi and Brussels there were no fortified places, and the fact that the main road nearly coincided with the dividing line between armies of different nationalities, customs and modes of speech, would prove of no little advantage.

The roads between Charleroi and the frontier were certainly in bad condition, having been broken up at the commencement of the Hundred days, but once across the Sambre there were but thirty-four miles of a good chaussée between Napoleon and Brussels. By deciding to advance on the line of demarcation between the cantonments of the Allies, it was at once apparent that the first blow would fall on Prussian troops. The corps of Zieten formed the outpost line, and the remaining Prussian corps were placed so as to readily concentrate and cover its retirement. Blücher might possibly evade a battle by retiring to unite with Wellington, but if he did make a stand, it was in the natural course of things that he would fight near Sombreffe for the preservation of his direct line of communication with his ally. The disposition of the Anglo-Dutch forces, and the cautious character of Wellington, rendered it improbable that any serious opposition would be offered by him in the Fleurus triangle at an early stage in the operations.

The Plan of Campaign — Basing his plan on the above calculations, Napoleon decided to assemble his forces with the greatest secrecy south of Charleroi, cross the Sambre in its vicinity, and defeat any troops of Blücher that made a stand, before they could be assisted by their allies. Were the Prussians to assemble in force, a defeat would force them to retire on their own line of communications, and, by thus separating them from the Anglo-Dutch army, create an opportunity for new combinations and an advance on Brussels.

Concentration at Beaumont — The orders for concentration and movement to the frontier of the French Army of the North were issued early in June. Four army corps of a strength of 80,000 men lay at Lille, Valenciennes, Mezières and Metz, while 45,000 men, including a cavalry corps, were in the vicinity of Paris, Soissons and Laon. The movement of the troops northwards from Paris would not excite comment, as it was but natural that the French army should assemble so as to meet the Allied advance. To close in from the flanks without revealing the place of concentration was a more difficult matter.

The greatest secrecy in movement was enforced; an embargo was placed on all information passing between France and Belgium, National Guards and Volunteers gradually replaced the regular troops in the vicinity of the frontier, and demonstrations were made wherever possible against the enemy's outpost force to the westward. But little was revealed to the army corps leaders, who were simply told their respective destinations, and warned not to discuss the situation with their subordinates. Gérard was ordered to leave Metz on June 6 for Phillippeville, and to close the gates of the fortress, and allow no communication with the outer world. Similarly, the troops at Lille and Valenciennes were directed on Avesnes and Maubeuge, in ignorance of the part they were to play in future operations.

The whole movement was admirably planned, and on the evening of June 14 the Army of the North (with the exception of a portion of Gérard's corps) was assembled at Solre-sur-Sambre, Beaumont, and Phillippeville, in close proximity to the Prussian outpost line. Even at this early stage in the operations the defects of a hastily improvised staff became apparent. The march movement of Gérard was miscalculated, and the cavalry of Grouchy were only able to get to the place of assembly by forced marches—a bad preparation for the opening of the campaign. It is also clear that Napoleon intended Vandamme's corps to form up at Phillippeville with the corps of Gérard, but that a defect in Soult's orders prevented this result being attained. The centre column was therefore increased in number by 17,000 to 18,000 men.

L. V. 224

Ordre du Jour, Avesnes, June 13

Elaborate instructions had been issued as to the situations of the bivouacs, and their formation in several lines. All watch fires were to be suppressed, and precautions taken that no one should leave the camp in the direction of the enemy. The troops were to be provided with four days' rations and fifty rounds of ammunition, and all were to be ready to move by 3 a.m. on the morning of June 15. There were no good roads between the frontier and the Sambre, and the corps, in their advance to the river,

THE PLAN OF CAMPAIGN

were enjoined to utilize every passage, and to move on a broad front in as close order as possible.

À l'armée, Avesnes, June 14 — On the evening of the 14th there was read out to the soldiers one of those stirring proclamations with which the Emperor was ever wont to herald the opening of a campaign.

Ordre de Movement, Beaumont, June 14 — The marching orders for the advance on Charleroi were not issued till late at night, and have been justly praised for their clearness and mastery of detail. According to modern views, they contain a great deal of matter which might be with advantage left to the discretion of the corps commanders. But this only emphasizes the fact prominently brought to notice in many later episodes of the campaign, of how entirely the French army was dominated by the personality of Napoleon.

Attitude of the Allies — The concentration of the French forces on the frontier did not escape the observation of the Allied outposts. On June 12, Dornberg, commanding the cavalry near Mons, reported that there were 100,000 men between Avesnes and Phillippeville. On the night of the 13th, the light reflected upon the sky by the French bivouac fires marked the position of great camps at Solre and Beaumont, and Zieten ordered his heavy baggage to be sent off to Gembloux. News of the arrival on the scene of Napoleon in person, and the reports from the outposts on the 14th, made it apparent that an attack was imminent. The corps of Zieten had detailed instructions as to making an obstinate resistance before falling back on Fleurus, while Blücher, at midday, sent orders to his other three corps to con-

H. 116 R. 70

centrate preparatory to a general advance in the same direction.

Wellington adhered to the view that Napoleon would advance, if at all, by way of Mons, or to the westward of it, and judging his troops to be well placed to meet such an eventuality, was careful not to make any premature movement. "The two commanders no doubt intended to act in concert, but there was not any definite agreement as to the particular steps to be taken in the event of a French invasion." In fact, they neither of them thought it probable. Blücher, a few days before, wrote to his wife: "Bonaparte will never attack"; while Wellington, in a letter dated June 15, calmly expressed to the Czar his intention of taking the offensive at the end of the month.

R. 72

H. 109

Views of Napoleon

In view of the controversy—hereafter to be dealt with—as to the strategy of invasion, and the importance of seizing the strategic points of Sombreffe and Quatre-Bras, it is as well to collect here the evidence as to what was the opinion of Napoleon on the eve of hostilities. On June 14 he writes to his brother Joseph: "To-morrow I go to Charleroi, where the Prussian army is; that will occasion either a battle or the retreat of the enemy." To Davout he states: "I shall pass the Sambre to-morrow, the 15th. If the Prussians do not retire, we shall have a battle." On the night of the 14th–15th, reports were received from spies that everything was tranquil at Namur, Brussels and Charleroi, and it was clear that on the morning of the 15th no great alteration would have taken place in the positions of the Allied forces. On the other hand, Zieten would know

R. 45

of the presence in force of the French army, and it was quite possible that, when his outposts were driven in, he might elect to concentrate and make a stand in the neighbourhood of Charleroi. The instructions given in the marching orders to Reille, Vandamme and Gérard, to arrive simultaneously and in battle formation before Charleroi, can only be explained by assuming that Napoleon expected a serious resistance at this point. The orders to the pioneers, engineer train and pontoon detachment, were evidently issued in anticipation of the bridges over the Sambre being destroyed. Even when the original orders were modified as the situation became more clear, the result was that over 100,000 men were directed to pass the Sambre by two narrow defiles at Charleroi and Marchiennes. "The intention of his Majesty is that the Sambre should be crossed before noon, and the army passed over to the left bank of the river."

But the movement was carried out with the utmost deliberation. There was no use made of several of the existing small bridges, nor any attempt to forward the movement by the formation of bridges of boats or pontoons. So far the evidence tells against the theory of a forced march with the intention of seizing two points on the distant Namur-Nivelles road. The orders show that early on the 15th the left wing was destined to pursue the north road towards Quatre-Bras, while the main force had necessarily to follow up the retreat of Zieten, and be in a position to deal with any force of Prussians that might be assembled. There was little probability of any Anglo-Dutch force, beyond

<small>Quatre-Bras to Charleroi, 12 miles</small>

<small>Sombreffe to Charleroi, 11 miles</small>

THE WATERLOO CAMPAIGN

outpost troops, being encountered, while it was an open question as to whether Blücher would make a stand or retire. In any case the situation would have to be cleared up by an advance in the direction of Fleurus and Gembloux.

THE CONTENDING ARMIES

CHAPTER III

The Contending Armies

The French Army—The Anglo-Dutch Army—The Prussian Army—Numbers and Positions of the Armies on the 14th of June.

The French Army — The army which Napoleon was about to lead on a desperate enterprise numbered some 124,000 men, of whom 90,000 were infantry. The battalions did not, as a rule, exceed 500 men, while the squadrons were 125 strong. To each division of infantry was attached a battery of 6-pounder guns with two howitzers, while each army corps had in addition a battery of 12-pounders. The mounted batteries attached to the cavalry divisions consisted of four 6-pounder guns with two howitzers. The Imperial Guard, in addition to its usual complement of batteries, had 52 guns in reserve.

The cavalry and artillery of the force were well organized and in good condition, but the infantry—with the exception of the Imperial Guard—in many points displayed weakness. The brigades, divisions and corps had only recently been formed, and in the newly raised units the officers and men were strangers to one another and unaccustomed to act in concert. The hastily formed Staff were weak in numbers, and unequal to their work.

But the main defect of the force was the lack of discipline. The soldiery had within the short space of a year seen their chief officers renounce Napoleon in favour of the Bourbons, and again betray the King to return to their former leader. The very devotion they had for the Emperor made them more suspicious of those whose principles were so unstable. Treason was everywhere scented, and the simplest movement or order was viewed with the utmost suspicion. Nor were the relations of the officers amongst themselves more satisfactory. Fame, fortune and place were at stake, bickering and jealousies were rampant, and the more far-seeing had little confidence in the ultimate issue of the campaign. The genius of the Emperor might command a temporary success, but France, exhausted in men, material and money, could not long withstand the vast resources of a European coalition. Afraid to go forward, unwilling to draw back, it was with a half-hearted effort that their great leader was followed.

H. 84 "Such was the army of 1815—impressionable, critical, without discipline, and without confidence in its leaders. . . . Haunted by the dread of treason, it was nevertheless instinct with warlike aspirations. . . . It was capable of heroic efforts and furious impulses. Napoleon had never before handled an instrument of war which was at once so formidable and so fragile." Though not the best army he had ever led, it was still a force superior to that possessed by either of his adversaries.

Anglo-Dutch Army In strong contrast with the Army of the North was the motley force led by Wellington. Of the 100,000 men who took the field, barely a third were British; and, mixed with the veterans of the Peninsula, were a large number of recruits, while many of the battalions were new and hastily raised. The King's German Legion, some 6,000 strong, were troops of the highest quality. Good work might be expected of the Brunswick contingent, while the Hanoverians were raw troops, formed mostly in landwehr regiments. The fidelity of the Nassau and Dutch-Belgian troops was strongly suspected; all the generals and most of the regimental officers of the latter had served in the French army, and the sympathies of the soldiers were supposed to be with Napoleon. On the other hand, the cavalry and artillery of the British and the Legion were probably the best in the field, and the force, imperfect as it was, contained many elements of strength. The Duke himself was feared and trusted, and the stern discipline enforced welded a mass of heterogeneous elements into an army which, for defensive fighting, was of undoubted value. It would have been hazardous, probably, to manœuvre to any great extent under fire a force which, in a passive attitude, would not flinch from a cannonade or serious attack. A weak and inexperienced Staff increased the difficulties of command, and it was only a victorious issue that has buried in oblivion many a serious defect.

Prussian Army The Prussian army of 123,000 men was composed of about two-thirds regular troops and one-third landwehr. Veterans and recruits were, however, alike of one tongue and one race, and moved by the same patriotic fervour. In every Frenchman they saw a mortal enemy, and a fanatic hatred of the despot who had so many times defeated them filled all ranks with a fierce resentment. Though the cavalry and artillery were inferior to those of the French, the infantry were probably better than that of the foe, though unequal to the veterans of the Imperial Guard. To their chief, "Marshal Vorwarts," they were, probably, as devoted as the old French soldiers were to Napoleon, and they had an entire confidence in their Staff and generals.

The situation and numbers of the Allied armies on June 14, before active hostilities took place, and the strength of the invading force, may be summed up as follows:—

The Army under Napoleon

THE FRENCH ARMY

1st Corps (D'Erlon)
- 1st Division (Alix)
- 2nd Division (Donzelot)
- 3rd Division (Marcognet)
- 4th Division (Durutte)
- 33 battalions
- 1st Cavalry Division (Jacquinot) . 11 squadrons
- 19,839 men
- 46 guns

2nd Corps (Reille)
- 5th Division (Bachelu)
- 6th Division (Jerome Bonaparte)
- 7th Division (Girard)
- 8th Division (Foy)
- 42 battalions
- 2nd Cavalry Division (Piré) . 15 squadrons
- 25,134 men
- 46 guns

3rd Corps (Vandamme)
- 9th Division (Lefol)
- 10th Division (Habert)
- 11th Division (Berthezène)
- 31 battalions
- 3rd Cavalry Division (Domon) . 10 squadrons
- 17,429 men
- 38 guns

4th Corps (Gérard)	12th Division (Pécheux) 13th Division (Vichery) 14th Division (Bourmont) 7th Cavalry Division (Maurin)	26 battalions 14 squadrons	16,634 men 38 guns
6th Corps (Lobau)	19th Division (Simmer) 20th Division (Jeannin) 21st Division (Teste)	20 battalions	10,490 men 38 guns
Imperial Guard	1st Division (Friant) 2nd Division (Moraud) Young Guard (Duhèsme) Light Cavalry Division (Lefèbre-Desnouettes) Heavy Cavalry Division (Guyot)	23 battalions 26 squadrons	19,909 men 96 guns
Reserve Cavalry (Grouchy)	1st Corps (Pajol) 2nd Corps (Exelmans) 3rd Corps (Kellermann) 4th Corps (Milhaud)	24 squadrons 31 squadrons 25 squadrons 24 squadrons	13,544 men 48 guns

[1] Total, in round numbers = 123,035 officers and men
350 guns

---

[1] The numbers are taken from De Bas, who gives the state of each corps in great detail. According to Lettow-Vorteck the numbers are 122,408, while Houssaye gives 124,139 men with 370 guns. Ropes by deducting wagon train, etc., arrives at a tolerably correct total, but the detail of combatants is obviously inaccurate. It seems probable that not more than 344 guns advanced beyond Charleroi.

The Anglo-Dutch Army

The Army under Wellington

1st Corps (Prince of Orange) H.Q. Braine-le-Comte	1st Division (Cooke)	Enghien (H.Q.) and neighbourhood	4,061	24,864 inf. 56 guns
	3rd Division (Alten)	Soignies (H.Q.) and neighbourhood	6,970	
	2nd D.B. Division (Perponcher)	Nivelles (H.Q.) and towards Charleroi-Brussels road	7,444	
	3rd D.B. Division (Chassé)	Roeulx and towards Binche	6,389	
2nd Corps (Lord Hill) H.Q. Ath	2nd Division (Clinton)	Ath (H.Q.), Lens, Leuze	6,883	23,568 inf. 40 guns
	4th Division (Colville)	Oudenarde (H.Q.) Renaix and west of Scheldt	7,212	
	1st D.B. Division (Stedmann)	Sotteghem (H.Q.) and villages between Ghent, Grammont and Alost	6,171	
	D.I. Brigade	. . . . . .	3,352	
Reserve (Wellington) H.Q. Brussels	5th Division (Picton)	Brussels . . .	7,158	20,517 inf. 64 guns
	6th Division (Cole)	Brussels neighbourhood and Hal	5,149	
	Brunswick Corps (Duke of Brunswick)	Brussels to Malines	5,376	
	Nassau Contingent (Kruse)	Brussels to Louvain	2,834	

THE CONTENDING ARMIES

Cavalry (Lord Uxbridge)	British and German Legion	Ninove, Grammont, Ghent, and valley of Dender Two regiments to frontier, near Tournai, Ypres.	8,473	14,315 cav. 44 guns
	Brunswick Cavalry	Brussels	922	
	Hanoverian Cavalry	Mons to Tournai	1,682	
	Dutch-Belgian Brigade	Roeulx, Mons, Binche and frontier	3,238	

Artillery, Engineers, and Park   9,708

[1] TOTAL=92,972 men
with 204 guns
or with officers and sergeants about 100,000 officers and men

Army under Blucher

THE PRUSSIAN ARMY.

1st Corps (Zieten)	1st Division (Steinmetz)	Fontaine l'Evêque and frontier from Binche to Sambre	35,568 men 88 guns
	2nd Division (Pirch, II)	Charleroi (H.Q.), and the Sambre bridges from La Roux to Châtelet	
	3rd Division (Jagow)	Fleurus and Sambre bridges at Farciennes, Tamines	
	4th Division (Henkel)	Moustier and along river in vicinity	
	Reserve Cavalry	Gosselies	

The outpost troops of the 1st Corps were extended along the frontier, from the south-west of Binche to Sosoye with supports at Lobbes, Thuin, Ham-sur-Heure, and Gerpinnes.

---

[1] The above figures are those of Sibborne corrected by reference to De Bas, and include only the rank and file of the British and K.G. Legion. There were besides 12,845 garrison troops, making a total of 105,517 men. The total force including officers amounted to 110,488 men with 220 guns. (De Bas) vide App. xx.

2nd Corps (Pirch, I)	5th Division 6th Division 7th Division 8th Division Reserve Cavalry Outpost Troops	Namur (H.Q.) Near Perwez Heron Huy Hannut Sosoye to Dinant	33,048 men 80 guns
3rd Corps (Thielemann)	9th Division 10th Division 11th Division 12th Division Reserve Cavalry Outpost Troops	Assesse Ciney (H.Q.) Dinant Huy Between Ciney and Dinant Dinant to Rochefort	25,318 men 48 guns
4th Corps (Bulow)	13th Division 14th Division 15th Division 16th Division Reserve Cavalry	Liège (H.Q.) Warremme Hologne Liers Trond, Looz, Tongres	32,239 men 88 guns

[1] TOTAL—123,173 officers and men with 304 guns

---

[1] Lettow Vorbeck. The Prussian army corps were subdivided into brigades which corresponded in numbers to the divisions of the other armies, and are for convenience so called in the narrative. The force included 11,948 cavalry. Charras gives his reasons for thinking that these numbers are too small. From the details now given it will be apparent that at the commencement of hostilities the French and Prussian armies were as nearly as possible equal in numbers, and that the strength of the Anglo-Dutch field force has generally been underestimated.

THE PASSAGE OF THE SAMBRE—THE 15TH OF JUNE

CHAPTER IV

The Passage of the Sambre—The 15th of June

Position of the French Army—Positions of Zieten's Corps—Advance of Left Column—Advance of Central Column—Advance of Right Column—Position of Affairs at Noon—Advance of Left Column on Gosselies—Action at Gosselies—Arrival of Ney—Advance on Quatre-Bras—Action at Frasnes—Retreat of Prussians—Advance of Main Body—Action at Gilly—Was Ney Ordered to seize Quatre-Bras?—Comments.

Position of French Army On the evening of June 14, the Allies, though aware of the French concentration, lay tranquil in their cantonments, while the Army of the North was bivouacked in close proximity to the frontier in three groups:—

Left Column 45,000 men	{ 1st Corps (D'Erlon) .	Solre-sur-Sambre.
	{ 2nd Corps (Reille) .	Leers.
Central Column 62,000 men	{ 3rd Corps (Vandamme) { 6th Corps (Lobau) { Imperial Guard . . . . . { Reserve Cavalry (Grouchy)	Around Beaumont
Right Column 16,000 men	{ 4th Corps (Gérard)	Near Phillippeville

Positions of Zieten's Corps Guarding the river passages and the approaches to them was the corps of Zieten, whose outpost troops were everywhere in contact with those of the enemy. Early in May, Zieten issued orders to his brigadiers as to the course to pursue in case of a French advance. The general scheme of retirement was for the outpost troops to fall back on the Sambre bridges. The 2nd Division was to hold the passages at Marchiennes, Charleroi and Châtelet a sufficient time to enable the 1st Division to withdraw its outposts, and fall back eastwards in a line with it. The 3rd and 4th Divisions, after disputing the passage of the river, were to retire on Fleurus, where it was contemplated that the whole corps should assemble. The reserve cavalry and artillery were to fall back on Sombreffe and Gembloux. The Army Corps covered a front of some thirty-six miles, and the operation of retirement had to be timed with great nicety. The troops in front line had to make a sufficient resistance to enable rallying points in rear to be occupied, while to hold their positions too long would endanger the desired retreat.

Sketch I

The day broke fair on June 15, when the French advanced troops crossed the frontier. The order of movement prescribed a concentric advance of the three main columns on Charleroi, but a subsequent order directed the left wing to pass by the bridge of Marchiennes, and the right column by that of Châtelet.

Reille, leaving his bivouac at 3 a.m., pushed back the Allied outposts, and, with his advanced guard, attacked Thuin. The landwehr battalion holding the place was driven out after a gallant resistance, and forced to retire on Montigny, where, supported by two squadrons of Prussian dragoons, it made a brief stand. The small force threatened on all sides by the numerous French cavalry lost heavily, but eventually gained Marchi-

Advance of left Column

ennes, the barricaded bridge of which was held by a battalion and two guns. The attack was not pressed with vigour, and it was nearly twelve o'clock before the leading squadrons of the 2nd Corps defiled across the river in the direction of Jumet, where the troops halted for further orders. The Prussian detachment, when driven in, retired on Damprémy and Gilly; while, meantime, the 1st Division of Steinmetz was in process of movement from Fontaine l'Evêque on Gosselies.

D'Erlon, with the 1st Corps, was directed to follow Reille, occupy Thuin with a division, and construct têtes du pont at Thuin and Aulne. He was further enjoined to reconnoitre towards Mons and Binche. From reasons, hitherto unexplained, the commander of the 1st Corps was very late in breaking camp, and did not reach Marchiennes till after four o'clock in the afternoon. The delay of Reille at Marchiennes, and the slow movements of D'Erlon, are difficult to reconcile with the view that Napoleon had ever represented to them that he was making a forced march with the object of reaching the Nivelles-Namur road.

Advance of Central Column The advance of the main column was headed by cavalry, under Pajol, who, after driving in the outposts at Ham, arrived before Charleroi shortly after eight o'clock. A narrow dyke, some 300 paces in length, was the only approach to the bridge, which was barricaded and defended by a Prussian battalion. Infantry was required to carry the position, and Pajol looked back in vain for the troops of Vandamme, who were to act in his support. The 3rd Corps should have started at 3 a.m., but the solitary staff officer, who bore the orders, had fallen on the way, and it was only the pressure of Lobau's troops on the rear of the corps that eventually caused it to move at 7 a.m.[1] On learning of the delay, Napoleon hurried forward, by a bypath, a division of the Young Guard, which, with its sappers, made a rush for the bridge, and sweeping away the barricade, cleared the way for the squadrons of cavalry. The Prussian garrison effected their retreat in good order on Gilly, though hotly pursued by Pajol's dragoons. A regiment of hussars was at once sent forward along the Brussels chaussée to reconnoitre. It was now past noon, and the infantry of the main column were crossing the Charleroi bridge, and subsequently defiled past the Emperor with great cheering.

Advance of Right Column The corps of Gérard on the right was delayed, awaiting the arrival of one of its divisions; and further time was lost, owing to the agitation and disorder caused by the desertion to the enemy of General de Bourmont and his Staff. The corps did not assemble on the heights of Florenne till seven o'clock, and the advanced guard reached the undefended bridge at Châtelet about 3 p.m. The movement of the main body was very slow, owing to the want of good roads and the difficulties presented by the terrain.

Position at Noon Shortly after noon the position of affairs was briefly as follows: On the left the head of the 1st corps of Reille had crossed at Marchiennes, and was forming up on the main road south of Gosselies. In the centre, the cavalry of Pajol had

---

[1] This *funeste contretemps* is charged to the fault of Soult. The caustic remarks of Chesney are worth reading. Chesney, 88.

passed through Charleroi, and, sending one regiment down the Brussels road, with the remainder pursued the retiring Prussian battalions. On the right, the troops of Gérard were some miles south of Châtelet. The 1st Division (Steinmetz) of Zieten's corps was, meanwhile, crossing the Piéton, and retiring on Fleurus by way of Gosselies; while the 2nd Division, with the bulk of its troops, was assembling in a rear-guard position on the wooded heights which overlooked the Gilly valley.

Advance of Left on Gosselies The hussars, despatched by Pajol towards Brussels, were met a little beyond Jumet by Prussian cavalry. On the report reaching Napoleon, he at once sent orders to Reille (at Jumet) to advance on Gosselies, where the enemy was stated to be in force, and, shortly after, sent forward the light cavalry of the guard to assist the hussars, while a regiment of the guard and a battery of horse artillery were posted on the chaussée in support. D'Erlon was enjoined to recall the detachments he had left on the Sambre, and form up in rear of the 2nd Corps, while at the same time the approaches from Mons were to be carefully watched.

Action at Gosselies The advance of the French across the river at Marchiennes and Charleroi seriously threatened the retirement of the division of Steinmetz. Zieten, realizing the situation, detached westward from the 3rd Division at Fleurus a regiment of infantry and a regiment of cavalry to assist in covering the movement. It was this Prussian cavalry that checked the hussars of Pajol, and they were in turn driven back by Piré's lancers, who formed the advanced guard of Reille's corps.

On the arrival of the leading infantry of the 2nd Corps, Gosselies was captured, but Steinmetz, approaching from the westward, checked any further advance by a vigorous attack, and, under cover of troops posted in houses north of the town, made good his retreat to Heppignies.

The 7th Division (Girard) was sent by Reille in pursuit, but was unable to make any headway, and Steinmetz, without further difficulty, fell back on Fleurus.

Arrival of Ney

H. 121

While the above events were taking place, Ney—about 3 p.m.—appeared on the scene at Charleroi, and was given command of the 1st and 2nd Army Corps, and the cavalry that had been sent along the Brussels chaussée; and ordered to drive back any of the enemy that he might find on the main road to Brussels.[1] At about five o'clock, the Marshal, with but one Staff officer, overtook the left column in front of Gosselies.

Advance on Quatre-Bras, 5 p.m.

The road to Brussels appeared open, and there were no signs of Anglo-Dutch troops. There were still four hours of daylight, and it was possible to push forward a strong advanced guard and occupy Quatre-Bras. Ney, however, unprovided with a Staff, suddenly put in command of a force in which many of the officers and men distrusted him, appears to have lost his wonted daring and self-confidence. Where rashness might have been excused, he reverted to extreme prudence. Already the left column had advanced far from the main body, and the sound

---

[1] Houssaye and Ropes maintain the view that there was also a formal order to occupy Quatre-Bras. The question is discussed later on.

THE PASSAGE OF THE SAMBRE 39

of firing in the Fleurus direction (at Gilly) denoted that a serious engagement was taking place. The corps of D'Erlon extended from Jumet as far back as the Sambre, and prudence suggested a preliminary concentration of his command. Instead, therefore, of at once continuing his march, the Marshal contented himself with sending Bachelu's division and Piré's cavalry to Mellet, while the remaining divisions of the 2nd Corps were posted round Gosselies. Along the chaussée to Brussels there was sent forward alone the cavalry of Lefebre-Desnouettes, with a complete disregard to the instructions of Napoleon as to its employment.

H. 122

Action at Frasnes

On approaching Frasnes, about 5.30 p.m., the lancers were checked by the fire of a battery of horse artillery, which, together with a Nassau battalion, was occupying the village. The leading battalion of Bachelu's division, which had reached Mellet, hurried forward in support and attacked in front, while the cavalry, pressing on the flanks, reached Quatre-Bras with one of its squadrons.[1] The defenders of Frasnes, meanwhile, fell back slowly on the woods of Bossu, in front of Quatre-Bras, where a welcome support of four battalions from Genappe had arrived at a critical moment. Ney, reconnoitring the position, considered it impossible to carry it with cavalry supported by a single battalion, and, as darkness was falling, rallied the attacking force at Frasnes, and returned himself to Gosselies. Later, he either rode to Charleroi and had an interview [2] with the

H. 130

---

[1] A patrol reached Sart-a-Mavelines. L.V. 298.
[2] Heymès is the sole authority for this (R. 116), but many of his statements have been proved to be untrustworthy. Ney makes no

Emperor, or, as is more probable, contented himself with sending a report.

Retreat of Prussians When the Prussian troops fell back from Marchiennes, Le Roux and Charleroi, they were formed up by General Pirch II, in a rearguard position on the wooded heights that overlooked the Gilly stream. Four battalions and a battery, well under cover, occupied an extended line from Soleillemont to Châtelinau. A regiment of dragoons formed the advanced posts, and watched the valley of the Sambre from Châtelinau to Farciennes. Four battalions formed a reserve (the remaining battalion of the division being on the march to Fleurus from Damprémy). On the road between Farciennes and Lambusart were half the 3rd Division of Jagow, four regiments of cavalry, and two batteries.

Advance of the Main Body Before the position the cavalry of Pajol was checked, and Grouchy, who had arrived on the scene, galloped back to the Emperor and reported that the enemy were 20,000 strong. Napoleon undertook a reconnaissance in person, and justly estimating the force not to exceed 10,000 men, **About 3.30 p.m.** arranged the plan of attack with Grouchy, to whom he verbally gave command of the right wing of the army. One of the divisions of Vandamme, whose corps was passing through Charleroi, was, in conjunction with Pajol, to make a frontal attack, while the two brigades of Exelmans' cavalry corps were to take the enemy in flank. The Emperor then retired

mention of it in his letter to the Duke of Otranto, and in his letter of 7 a.m. of June 16 he refers to a report and makes no mention of an interview. H. 136.

to Charleroi to hasten the advance of Vandamme's corps. Grouchy and Vandamme occupied two hours in arranging the attack, and Napoleon, surprised at not hearing the sound of the guns, returned to the field, and shortly after six o'clock ordered an immediate advance. After a sharp artillery fire, the attack was made in three columns. The Prussians, having closed the Fleurus road with abattis, did not await the shock. Napoleon, enraged at seeing his enemy escape, ordered his escort of four squadrons to pursue, and fall on the retiring infantry. Two of the Prussian battalions had gained the wood of Soleillemont, but the others were taken at a disadvantage, and suffered severely. On the southern flank the dragoons of Exelmans drove back the Prussian cavalry, and forced the infantry back on Lambusart, where General Pirch rallied his troops and made a stand. Pressed vigorously by the numerous French horsemen, the Prussians retired through Fleurus, leaving the village occupied by only two battalions, and rejoined the remaining divisions of Zieten's corps in the vicinity of Ligny. Vandamme, stating that his troops were too tired to pursue, bivouacked in the Soleillemont woods, covered in front line by the cavalry of Exelmans and Pajol.

Action at Gilly

The admirable defence made by Zieten is generally praised, and the dexterity with which his divisions extricated themselves from a difficult position is worthy of study. By delaying his retreat too long, Steinmetz certainly exposed his troops to a heavy loss, but the chief error was that Zieten did not make proper arrangements to blow up the Sambre bridges.[1] No sufficient

[1] The Duke at Paris commented on the lack of experience in such matters of the Prussian Engineers.

explanation has ever been given of this default. A matter of even greater importance was, however, the transmission of intelligence of the enemy's movements to the Allied Head Quarters with the greatest despatch. As will be afterwards seen, the arrangements made by the Prussian Staff were very defective, and entailed serious consequences.

Was Ney ordered to Seize Quatre-Bras? The wording of the verbal order given to Ney has been disputed. Was he definitely told to occupy Quatre-Bras? The evidence is very conflicting, and in such cases it is wisest to consider the situation at the moment. It was past three o'clock in the afternoon when the order was given; half the army was still south of the Sambre, and Grouchy had reported that there was a force of 20,000 men in front of him. Overestimated as the enemy might be, it was clear that Zieten's corps was retiring on the Fleurus road. An advance on Sombreffe would certainly be disputed, and the cavalry of Grouchy would be unable to push forward till supported by infantry. The advance of the main body was temporarily checked, and it would require the rest of the day to amass sufficient troops for a forward movement to any distance. Is it possible that under the circumstances Napoleon would order his left wing to occupy in force with his left column a position 12 miles distant? On the other hand, the Emperor knew perfectly well that D'Erlon had not yet crossed the Sambre and that at nightfall the command of Ney would be strung out from the river along the Brussels road. Was it not natural in a verbal order to say occupy Quatre-Bras, but in the sense that cavalry should do so with a view to gaining information and not with the intention of holding the cross-roads against the attack of the Anglo-Dutch army.[1]

Comments
The strategical situation at the outset of hostilities has been the subject of much comment. Napoleon is described as wishing to interpose between the two armies of the Allies, to wedge himself in between them with the object of separating them, to effect a strategical rupture or (phrase uncouth to English ears) to make a strategic penetration.

The vague phraseology of the strategist is often apt to obscure the simplest truths. If it be assumed that the armes of the Allies were sufficiently concentrated for fighting, and were advancing on either side of the Dyle district for the purpose of falling upon the invader, most of the recognized views on the strategical problem presented by the Fleurus triangle would be understood. The importance of the early possession of Quatre-Bras and Sombreffe would be undoubted, and the ability of Napoleon in a central position to manœuvre so as to defeat each army in succession would be admitted.[2] But to Napoleon the situation presented a very different aspect. On June 14, he knew that the Allies in

---

[1] The bulletin of June 15 makes it clear that at Head Quarters there was an opinion that under favourable circumstances some troops might reach Quatre-Bras. R. 61-9.; H. 123, 526; L.V. 264; G. 35.

[2] Had Napoleon under the actual circumstances seized Quatre-Bras and Sombreffe in force on the evening of the 15th, an interesting problem would have arisen. The Allies had agreed to act in concert, and their most natural course was for Wellington to take up position at Hal and Waterloo, while Blücher retired on Wavre. Zieten would fall back on his main army, and had Blücher decided to give battle he would undoubtedly do so near Gembloux, at which point the Emperor could not concentrate his troops till late on the afternoon

their widely extended cantonments had not moved a man. On the 15th, he could assume with confidence that there would not be at Quatre-Bras any Anglo-Dutch force of importance. He had alone to do with the Army Corps of Zieten, which in its retirement would fall back on the whole or portion of the other Prussian corps, who would of necessity move in the general direction of Gembloux and Sombreffe. Whether Blücher made a stand or not, it was upon his troops that the first blow must fall, and his defeat or retreat would enable the Emperor, with his main body, to afterwards attack Wellington on the Charleroi-Brussels chaussée. To ward off the attack of the widely dispersed and slowly moving troops of Wellington it would be advisable, but not absolutely necessary, to occupy Quatre-Bras on the 15th, while the distance to be traversed, and the obstacles to be overcome, rendered it clearly impossible that Sombreffe could be reached.

R. 58   There is no sufficient reason for distrusting Napoleon's own statement that he did not intend to occupy Sombreffe in force. The verbal order to Grouchy to pursue the enemy to Sombreffe was given, late in the afternoon of June 15, to a cavalry general, who had in front of him a strong rear-guard position, behind which the whole of Zieten's corps was retiring. It was simply a guiding direction as to how the pursuit was to be pressed, and not a definite order to carry out an impossibility. His reference to Ligny

---

of the 16th. The mere possession of the Nivelles-Namur road on the night of the 15th would not lead to the divergent retreat of the Allies, and on any other supposition the situation would be much less favourable to Napoleon than that which his foresight had produced. Cf. Grouard, Ropes and Houssaye.

may be an afterthought, but the whole tenor of his actions on the 15th, and the leisurely movements of the main body across the Sambre and towards Gilly, tend to show that, in his opinion, there was no necessity for pushing his infantry beyond Fleurus.

In summing up the strategical situation on the evening of June 15, it may be admitted that incomplete arrangements and an indifferent Staff service caused much delay; but this was undoubtedly lessened by the fact that none of the Sambre bridges were destroyed.

R. 53 As a general result, some 100,000 men were across the river, and the Emperor states that his manœuvres had succeeded to his wishes; he had it thenceforth in his power to attack the armies of the enemy in detail. In front of Fleurus he had a sufficient force wherewith he could overcome the Prussians if, as he thought it not unlikely, they should risk a battle on the next day. By the occupation of Quatre-Bras the next morning he would prevent Blücher from receiving any assistance from his Allies if they were in a position to afford it. As a matter of fact, Wellington, on June 15, had not moved a man to meet the enemy.

BLÜCHER AND WELLINGTON—THE 15TH OF JUNE

CHAPTER V

BLÜCHER AND WELLINGTON—THE 15TH OF JUNE

Blücher's Dispositions—Comments—Wellington's Dispositions—
Dutch-Belgian Movements—Comments.

Blücher's Dispositions

As early as the night of June 13, Zieten had reported the assembly of a large French force on the frontier. At midday on the 14th orders were sent to Bülow to concentrate at Hannut, and to the other corps to begin assembling and to be ready for any eventuality. Further information as to the threatening aspect of affairs was received from spies and deserters by Blücher in the afternoon, and the same night orders were issued for the 2nd, 3rd and 4th Corps to concentrate and march on Sombreffe. The 1st Corps was directed to make as obstinate a resistance as possible and fall back on Fleurus. The arrangements of the Staff for the transmission of orders were so defective that although Bülow was only thirty-five miles distant, the first dispatch took seventeen hours, and the second twelve hours, to reach him. The directions for a concentration at Sombreffe were issued at midnight on June 14, and the information, by means of the line of relays, should have reached Wellington in the early morning of the 15th. The omission to send a report to Brussels has never been explained. The second message from Zieten, in which

L. V. 199

he states that the French are advancing on both banks of the Sambre, reached Namur at eleven o'clock, and at midday a dispatch was sent to Müffling informing him of the news from the frontier and the concentration for battle of the Prussian army. A further order was sent to Bülow that he must start at latest in the very early morning of the 16th for Gembloux. Blücher now rode out to Sombreffe, where he arrived at four o'clock in the afternoon.

L. V. 270

Some two months previously he had examined the ground near Ligny, and had decided on the position to be taken up in the event of the French crossing the Sambre near Charleroi.

In the evening he writes to the King of Prussia:

H. 145

"I shall concentrate my army to-morrow morning . . . I am without news from Wellington. At any rate, to-morrow will be the decisive day."

With his four corps assembled, the Marshal had little fear of Napoleon, and deemed himself invincible. "With my 120,000 Prussians I would undertake to take Tripoli, Tunis and Algiers, if there were not the sea to cross." If the whole French army, with a strength equal to his own, were to confront him, he had the advantage of a chosen position, and the certainty of some aid from Wellington. If, on the other hand, the Anglo-Dutch army were held in check by a portion of the French army, he could count on a considerable superiority in numbers over any force that could be sent against him. The statement that Blücher only decided to accept battle after receiving a formal promise from Wellington is not in accordance with facts. Arrangements had undoubtedly been made as to the course to be pursued in case France should be invaded, but no definite plan had been formulated as to concerted action in the case of Napoleon invading Belgium. The two commanders no doubt agreed to give each other mutual support as far as possible, and it appears that Wellington approved of the Prussian concentration near Sombreffe. "The dispositions of the Field-Marshal are excellent," he says to Müffling on the evening of the 15th; "but I cannot decide anything till I know what is going on in the direction of Mons." The English commander had the difficult task of guarding all the approaches to the west of the marshy district traversed by the Dyle, and he did not commit himself to any definite statement as to what he would do until all doubt was removed as to the movements of the French army. But the occupation of Sombreffe forced his hand to the extent that, when the fog of war lifted, he had to move towards Quatre-Bras in support of his ally. Blücher undoubtedly looked to Wellington for aid, but he deliberately took up the Ligny position, knowing that support was uncertain, so confident was he in his ability to deal single-handed with the French forces.

H. 147

Comments

Had the Allied armies taken measures to concentrate on June 13, when it was known that the French were at Beaumont, a position held by Prussians at Sombreffe, with the Anglo-Dutch in force near Quatre-Bras, would clearly be of great strategical value. But under the existing circumstances there was grave danger in the attempt to assemble at a point within striking distance of an energetic enemy. According to Napoleon, Blücher ought to have retired on Wavre, where an undisturbed concentration of his whole army could have been effected. Even at Gembloux, as events turned out, it would have been possible to give battle, but the risk of taking up a position at Ligny is very evident from the fact of Napoleon's surprise in finding the main Prussian force to be disputing his advance.

The action taken by Blücher was clearly to the advantage of the Anglo-Dutch army. In order that the Allies might give battle in combination, it was necessary that the Prussians should either make a stand in the vicinity of Sombreffe or retire on Wavre. By electing the former course the whole Prussian Army acted as a magnet to the invading force, and gave Wellington the much needed time to assemble his widely extended divisions. Had the Prussians retired, the bulk of Napoleon's force might have at once proceeded on the main road to Brussels, and created a situation of great difficulty. It is quite possible that time would not have allowed of the taking up of a position at Waterloo, or of making a flank movement to concentrate on Wavre. Pressed in front by a superior force, an army striving to concentrate would probably have to fall back through the Soignes forest to the vicinity of Brussels before giving battle.

Wellington's Dispositions The immobility of Wellington on June 15 requires some explanation. Zieten states that he despatched a message at 4 a.m. that his outposts were attacked, but by some unexplained error the report did not reach Brussels till 3 p.m. At about this time the Prince of Orange rode in with the news that at an early hour there was heavy firing in the direction of Thuin. It appears also that Steinmetz, at 8 a.m., reported his retirement to Van Merlen, his nearest Belgian neighbour, but this, as well as the information sent in by the cavalry near Mons, was apparently delayed at the Head Quarters of the Prince of Orange. These were but the alarms from an outpost line; there was no certainty that the main French army was crossing the Sambre at Charleroi. A second report from Zieten despatched after eight o'clock did little to clear up the situation, and Wellington, always solicitous about his right, simply issued orders (between 6 and 7 p.m.) for his divisions to concentrate.

L. V. 284

Hart 53, 64 Later in the evening news was received announcing the proposed concentration of Blücher near Sombreffe, and also that no enemy was to be found in front of Mons. A second after-order was accordingly issued about 10 p.m., and the combined effect of these orders was, briefly, that of the 1st Corps three divisions were assembling at Nivelles, and the 4th was on the road to it at Braine-le-Comte. The 2nd Corps was being moved up from all sides to Enghien, while the reserves were assembled at Brussels ready to march at a moment's notice. Whether a third set of orders were issued in the early morning of June 16 is a matter of much controversy. Wellington, in his official report of June 19, distinctly states: "I had directed the whole army to march on Quatre-Bras." At midnight on June 15–16 he informs Müffling that "Orders for the concentration of my Army at Nivelles and Quatre-Bras are already despatched." At 1 a.m. the report that the French had appeared at Quatre-

Bras reached the ballroom, and must have influenced the Duke as to the necessity of advancing troops to that point. To the Duke of Richmond, about 2 a.m. on the 16th, he states: "I have ordered my army to concentrate at Quatre-Bras, but we shall not stop him there; and if so, I shall fight here (at the same time passing his thumb over the position of Waterloo)." There is no existing record of any third set of orders, and any instructions that may have been given to de Lancey were lost with his other papers at Waterloo. A possible solution of the difficulty may be arrived at by studying the effects of the two first set of orders delivered. The 1st Corps was concentrating on Nivelles, the 2nd moving up to Enghien in support, and Quatre-Bras was a point some seven miles further east on the direct road, Enghien—Nivelles—Quatre-Bras, on which the bulk of the troops were travelling. Even troops at Hal would have to pass through Nivelles to reach Quatre-Bras. Take into consideration the momentous events of the night of the 15th; the chief Staff officers being at the Brussels ball, and the fact that two sets of orders had already been sent out; is it not possible that merely verbal orders to "Push on to Quatre-Bras" might have been deemed sufficient by de Lancey? Be the matter as it may, the British Staff gave its leader, on the 16th, a very misleading document showing the position the troops should be in at 7 a.m. on June 16, and the statements made therein clearly refer to a movement on Quatre-Bras, of which no recorded order exists.[1]

Max. II. 14

R. 86

---

[1] The whole controversy about the three sets of orders is ably dealt with by Ropes, in Chap. V. Houssaye attaches credit only

The Dutch-Belgian Movements The concentration of the Dutch-Belgian divisions at Nivelles, according to the written orders, meant the withdrawal of all troops from the road from Charleroi to Brussels. Owing to the "intelligent disobedience" of subordinates, the peril thus threatened was averted. As before stated, the brigade of Saxe-Weimar, which was cantoned on the road from Genappe to Frasnes, concentrated on the evening of the 15th at Quatre-Bras, in time to ward off the attack of Ney. The news of the action at Frasnes reached Braine-le-Comte about 10 p.m., and in the absence of the Prince of Orange at Brussels, his Chief of the Staff directed Perponcher to support the troops at Quatre-Bras with his other brigade. When the first order for concentration arrived from Brussels, it was forwarded to Nivelles with a note: "It is impossi-

H. 154 at Brussels to know the exact state of things here." Perponcher did not hesitate, but marched with Bylandt's brigade to Quatre-Bras, where the whole of his division was formed up on the morning of the 16th, a movement that Wellington subsequently complimented him on, though not in accordance with his own orders.

Comments The wide extension of the cantonments of the Allied armies has often been criticized. It must be remembered, however, that they were not unsuited to a forward advance into France, in combination with the projected movement of the other armies

---

to the two sets, of whose existence there is no doubt. The error made in the first order as to the Guards assembling at Ath instead of at their headquarters at Enghien is put right by the 10 p.m. order. See also Robinson, *Wellington's Campaigns*, 1906, where the subject is dealt with in detail.

of the coalition. Neither Wellington nor Blücher believed that the Emperor would dare to attack them. When it became evident that such a contingency was possible, it is generally agreed that " in place of waiting to see where the blow actually fell, the armies should have been instantly put in motion to assemble." As this was not done by the Anglo-Dutch army, a false situation was created by the concentration of Blücher on Ligny, which forced Wellington to form up as many of his troops as possible at Quatre-Bras, or leave his ally without support. That the strategical position created was a dangerous one was proved by the events of the following day. The omission of Gneisenau to afford information on the night of the 14th as to the Prussian march on Sombreffe created difficulties of which he himself was the first to complain.[1]

R. 96

No sufficient explanation has ever been given for the delay in forwarding to Wellington the reports from the outposts, nor the insufficiency of the information afforded to him by Zieten. Even as it was, the assembling of the Anglo-Dutch troops appears unduly delayed. But the situation, as it appeared to Wellington, was by no means clear. Had Napoleon advanced with his main body either by Charleroi, Mons or Tournai, the attack had to be met by the Anglo-Dutch army alone, and it was impossible for the Allies to combine. Even if advancing by Charleroi—as he did—it was by no means certain that his main army would not at once

---

[1] Si può anzi dire, che gran parte della responsabilità del cattivo andamento delle operazioni in guesto giorno e nel sequente, spetti al G. Gneisenau. Pollio, 151.

proceed down the Brussels road. In such an event a forward position, like Nivelles or Quatre-Bras, could not long be maintained, and Wellington's hesitation would be explained.

<small>Kennedy, 157</small> It has been maintained that the first object of the Emperor should have been the defeat, or forced retreat, of the Anglo-Dutch army. Whether this be true or not, the fact that such a course seemed possible to Wellington may afford an explanation as to his hesitation in concentrating his force on points far in advance of Brussels, and within his adversary's reach.

THE MORNING OF THE 16TH JUNE—THE FRENCH ARMY

CHAPTER VI

The Morning of the 16th June—The French Army

Napoleon at Charleroi—Orders to Ney—Orders to Grouchy—
Operations of Ney—Operations of Grouchy—Comments.

Napoleon at Charleroi

R. 54
H. 136

AFTER being assured that the Prussians were everywhere in retreat, the Emperor in the dusk of the evening of June 15 returned to Charleroi. From three in the morning till eight at night he had been in personal command, and had displayed unusual vigour and endurance. Reports as to the situations of the several units of the army reached Head Quarters at midnight.[1] Neither Grouchy nor Vandamme had arrived at Fleurus, which was held by two battalions of the rear-guard of Zieten. About half of Gérard's corps was across the river, while that of Lobau and the heavy cavalry of Milhaud was still on the right bank of the Sambre. Ney, on the left wing, reported that

---

[1] According to Heymes, Ney supped with Napoleon, and it is suggested that Grouchy was also present (R. 65, 116). It seems improbable that the Marshals would quit their commands at the close of a very exhausting day. There is no corroborative evidence of the midnight interview, and Heymes is not always trustworthy. Had Ney only left Napoleon at 2 a.m., it seems unlikely that the Emperor would despatch an officer to Frasnes at 4 a.m., to learn what Ney did or could report to him.

a small Anglo-Dutch force had been driven out of Frasnes, and that the 2nd Corps (Reille) was at and near Gosselies. The leading troops of the 1st Corps (D'Erlon) had reached Jumet, but there was some uncertainty as to whether about half the corps had yet crossed the Sambre.

H. 139

As early as 4 a.m. on the 16th, Napoleon sent an orderly officer to Frasnes to learn the news. The exact distribution of the troops of the left wing was not quite clear, and at 5 a.m. Soult (Chief of the Staff) wrote to Ney for further details, and at the same time informed him that Kellermann's cuirassiers (at Châtelineau) were ordered to Gosselies, and placed at his disposal. A little after 6 a.m. a letter was

H. 140

received from Grouchy stating that strong columns of the enemy were coming up the Namur road, and advancing on Bry and St. Amand. A confirmatory dispatch was subsequently sent in by Girard, who had advanced his division (of Reille's corps) to Wangenies.

Orders to Ney

The operation orders for June 16 were not issued till between 7 and 8 a.m., and, in accordance with his usual custom, were followed by explanatory letters addressed by the Emperor to his two Marshals.

1st Order (Soult). R. 381

Ney was to move the 1st and 2nd Corps, and Kellermann's cavalry, on Quatre-Bras, take up a position there, and reconnoitre towards Brussels and Nivelles. If not inconvenient, he was further to push a division, with cavalry, to Genappe, and another division to Marbais, to serve as a link with the force of Grouchy. He was warned that Grouchy was advancing on Sombreffe, while the Emperor with the Guard would be at Fleurus before noon.

Letter from Napoleon to Ney. R. 378 App. 1 "I will attack the enemy if I meet him, and clear the road up to Gembloux. There at 3 p.m., or perhaps in the evening, according to circumstances, I will decide what to do. My wish is, that immediately I have decided, you be ready to march on Brussels. I will support you with the Guard from either Sombreffe or Fleurus, and I should like to arrive at Brussels to-morrow morning (the 17th)." Ney was further informed of the division of the army into two wings and a reserve, and was enjoined to, as far as possible, spare the Guard cavalry.[1]

Orders to Grouchy. R. 382 App. 7 The orders and letter to Grouchy make the intentions of the Emperor still more clear, and were to the following effect: He was to move the corps of Vandamme and Gérard with his cavalry divisions—some 50,000 men—on Sombreffe. The 4th Corps was to march so as to avoid Fleurus, and not interfere with the advance of the Guard. "If the enemy is at Sombreffe I propose to attack him: I will attack him even at Gembloux, and carry the position. After the situation is clear at these points, I intend to march this night and operate against the English with my left wing. I will be between 10 and 11 o'clock at Fleurus. All my information is to the effect that the Prussians cannot oppose to us more than 40,000 men."

The Operations of Ney On the night of June 15, the force under Ney's command was échélonned from Frasnes to Thuin, while the heavy cavalry division,

---

[1] The force placed under Ney's command on June 16 consisted of the 1st and 2nd Army Corps (less Girard's division), the light

which was to join him, was still on the Sambre.[1] The movement ordered for the day had not been completed, and it was obviously desirable that the early hours of the 16th should be devoted to concentrating the troops, and disposing them in readiness to carry out the further orders of the Emperor. Frasnes was but five miles from Gosselies, where Reille had two divisions, and by 9 a.m. over 20,000 men might have been in position to attack Quatre-Bras, with a reserve of a portion of the 1st Corps at Gosselies.

H. 192

The Marshal, however, issued no instructions beyond warning Reille to be in readiness to march, and the early hours of daylight found both the divisions of the 2nd Corps resting in their bivouacs. "Ney was no longer the man he had been." The ardent and impetuous "red-head" gave place to the cautious and hesitating leader.

About 6.30 a.m. on the 16th, the letter from Soult, that Kellermann's cuirassiers were placed under his command, was received. Shortly after, Ney rode to Frasnes, leaving word with Reille, that if any orders from the Emperor should arrive in his absence, they were to be executed at once, and their contents communicated to D'Erlon. Some desultory fighting took place in the outpost line near Quatre-Bras, but no importance appears to have been attached to it, nor was there any attempt made to reconnoitre the enemy's position, or estimate his strength.

At about eleven o'clock the letter of Napoleon, and

cavalry of the Guard under Lefèbre-Desnouettes and the cavalry corps of Kellermann—a total of some 45,000 men.

[1] Near Châtelineau.

the first formal order of advance from Soult, reached Frasnes. Ney at once dictated the necessary detailed instructions for the movement, and from them it is very apparent that he counted on encountering but little resistance. While the 2nd Corps, covered by a cavalry division, was to march on Genappe and Quatre-Bras, the remainder of the force (with the exception of Piré's squadrons and a division to Marbais) was to take up position at Frasnes, two miles from the cross-roads. Napoleon, at a distance, gave instructions for a forward movement, but that Ney, actually in sight of the enemy, did no more than forward a detailed transcript of them to his troops, is a proof of how entirely dependent he was on the Emperor, and how completely he failed to realize the military situation.

H. 194

Badly as Ney seconded the Emperor, he was not himself well supported by his corps leaders. Reille at Gosselies saw the operation orders[1] at 10 a.m., and, instead of at once moving, asked for further instructions on the ground that he had received intelligence[2] of the appearance of a Prussian force at Bry.

The delay has been excused on the high authority of Jomini, but seems the no less justifiable. The assembly of Prussians beyond Fleurus would naturally be known to Napoleon, and Ney could not possibly be so well informed. The march from Gosselies was thus

[1] General Flahault showed Reille the orders when passing through Gosselies on his way to Frasnes.
[2] Reille at 9 a.m. received a report from Girard at Wangenies that Prussians were advancing on the Namur road near St. Amand. This report was forwarded to Charleroi, but apparently not to Ney (R. 121; H. 195). A similar report had been received by Napoleon from Grouchy in the early morning.

F

delayed, until, at 11.45 a.m., when a peremptory order arrived from Frasnes to start at once.

While Ney was awaiting the arrival of the 2nd Corps,[1] a second order from Soult reached him probably about 12.30 p.m. It informed Ney that a report had reached the Emperor that the enemy were assembling in considerable force at Quatre-Bras, and that he was to " unite the corps of Reille and D'Erlon, and the cavalry of Kellermann ; with these forces you ought to be able to beat and destroy any force of the enemy you may meet." It goes on to state that it is not very likely that Blücher has sent any troops to Quatre-Bras so that Ney would only have to deal with those coming from Brussels.

2nd Order (from Soult). R. 381 App. 3

Towards half-past one Reille, marching at the head of his troops, joined Ney, who was desirous of at once advancing against the wood of Bossu. More prudent counsels, however, prevailed, and it was not till two o'clock that the divisions of the 2nd Corps deployed for attack.

H. 198

To support the advance, Ney relied on the army corps of D'Erlon, which had been directed to follow up the 2nd Corps to Frasnes.

There is reason to believe that D'Erlon, with his whole corps, was at Jumet, and ready to march on the morning of the 16th. But the road in front of him was blocked by the 2nd Corps, and he had to wait until the rearmost troops of Reille were in

H. 204

---

[1] In his criticism on the detailed orders given by Ney to his own command, Ropes does not give sufficient weight to the fact that this second order from Soult did not arrive at Frasnes until after the orders of Ney were sent out (R. 124).

MORNING OF 16th JUNE—FRENCH ARMY

movement. It was not till nearly two o'clock that the vanguard of the 1st Corps reached Gosselies. A delay of an hour here took place, owing to a false report that a force of Anglo-Dutch troops were threatening his left at Chapelle-Herlaimont, and it was not till three o'clock that the march was resumed.

Operations of Grouchy — On the evening of June 15, Grouchy was compelled to halt before Fleurus, owing to the refusal of Vandamme to second him, and also on account of the lateness of the hour. In the early morning of the 16th, he made preparations for a forward movement, but seeing the advancing columns of the enemy in the distance, hesitated, and awaited further instructions. When the operation orders for the day arrived, about half-past nine, he was so dismayed by the display of the Prussian forces, that he limited himself to occupying Fleurus, which had been evacuated by the enemy at dawn.

The Emperor appeared on the scene about 11 a.m., and, pending the arrival of the troops in rear, took observations from an old windmill in the outskirts of the town, and afterwards rode along the outpost line.

Comments — The delay in movement of the French army on the morning of the 16th has been made the subject of severe criticism. The strategic plan was not altered. " A right impulse once given to an army, it is in a position to turn events not calculated on, or miscalculated, to advantage." **Hamley, 95** Had Fleurus been occupied on the 15th as intended, and had there not been undue delays in passing the Sambre, there is little doubt that the main army might have been concentrated on the morning of June 16.

At midnight, on the 15th, the Emperor was fairly well informed of the positions of his troops, and that, owing to the backwardness o fthe 1st Corps, the command of Ney would occupy several hours in assembling near Quatre-Bras. To attack and defeat the Prussians (a primary object) it was necessary that any possibility of their being assisted by an Anglo-Dutch force must be prevented. The advance on Sombreffe had to be delayed until a simultaneous movement should be effected towards Quatre-Bras. Otherwise, it would be necessary to risk a battle with the Prussians on the chance that Ney, with the 2nd Corps alone, could prevent their being assisted by the English. So far the delay of checking the advance in force of the main body beyond Fleurus may be justified. On the other hand, there seems little excuse for the late issue from Head Quarters of the operation orders for the day. Gérard, who was still crossing the Sambre in the early morning, did not receive his orders till half-past nine, while the delay that took place at Gosselies has already been noticed. Had the orders of Soult been issued at midnight, and, in accordance with the usual custom, reached the several corps by daylight, the left wing could by ten o'clock have occupied Frasnes in force, with the leading divisions of D'Erlon in support at Gosselies. On the right flank, at the same time, the infantry of Grouchy's command might have been concentrated east and south of Fleurus, ready for immediate advance as soon as the reserve was in a position to afford support.

R. 132

Wellington expressed the opinion, that the inactivity of Napoleon on the morning of the 16th was due to the necessity of not harassing the troops after their long marches of the past few days.¹ The Emperor also possibly counted on more vigour and initiative being shown by his subordinates, and that his corps leaders would, without further instructions, carry out the definite orders given them the previous day.

R. 139

Unfortunate as was the delay, its results were accentuated, as previously shown, by the relations that existed between Napoleon and his generals, and by the distrust with which the soldiery regarded their leaders.

That there was an unnecessary delay there is no doubt, but the blame need not be laid upon Napoleon alone, but fairly apportioned between him and his corps generals.

---

[1] Jomini, in common with many others, attributes the delays to the Emperor not being in good health (G. 53). But Houssaye strongly combats this view (H. 498).

THE MORNING OF THE 16TH JUNE—THE ALLIED ARMIES

CHAPTER VII

THE MORNING OF THE 16TH JUNE—THE ALLIED ARMIES

Wellington at Brussels—The De Lancey Memorandum—Concentration at Ligny—Negligence of Gneisenau—Meeting of Wellington and Blücher.

Wellington at Brussels

BRUSSELS was full of the partisans of Napoleon. The orders for the concentration of the army at Nivelles and Enghien had been issued on the evening of the 15th, and it seemed advisable to the Duke to tranquillize the well disposed by appearing with his Staff at the ball given by the Duchess of Richmond. It was after midnight when the news arrived that the French had appeared at Frasnes. The Prince of Orange at once set out for Genappes, and arriving at Quatre-Bras at 6 a.m. on June 16, found the Anglo-Belgian division of Perponcher in position. The Staff of the distant divisions silently slipped away from the ballroom, and instructions were sent, probably about 7 a.m., to Lord Hill at Enghien to forward as soon as possible the second division of infantry, and all the cavalry to Braine-le-Comte, and the Indian Brigade to Enghien. The Reserves were started in the early morning for Waterloo, where they halted at about 10 a.m. There is no further record of orders issued, but there is little doubt that the Duke,

R. 374

73

in the early morning, instructed his Staff that the troops moving on Nivelles should be pushed forward on Quatre-Bras, where he himself arrived at 10 a.m.

The Duke gave his approval to the action which Perponcher, on his own responsibility, had taken, and proceeded towards Frasnes for an inspection of the French outposts. At 10.30 a letter was written to Blücher, giving him to understand that the 1st Corps, the Reserves, and part of the 2nd Corps, would be assembled at the cross-roads in the early afternoon. It is evident that the Duke was labouring under a grave misconception as to the exact situation of his army. The "Disposition of the British Army at 7 a.m.,[1] June 16," written out for his information by Colonel de Lancey, is a document so absolutely incorrect that it is difficult to account for its issue. It was practically impossible that several of the divisions could have been at seven o'clock at the place where the Chief of the Staff said they were. For example, the 2nd Division of Clinton was not at Braine-le-Comte, but at Ath, some twenty-five miles off, and at seven o'clock had not received its marching orders! The Duke, however, apparently accepted the statements made without demur, and on the faith of the representations,

R. 85

R. 111

---

[1] This unsigned, undated memorandum was found among the Wellington papers, and the explanatory note at its foot was signed by Sir De Lacy Evans some years after the battle. It was apparently jotted down in the field on the road to Genappe, and was probably meant to be explained by word of mouth. Be the case as it may, there is no doubt that Wellington, when he wrote to Blücher from Frasnes, did not realize the exact situation of his troops. The details as to this memorandum, and the orders of Wellington, are ably analysed in Robinson's *Wellington's Campaigns*, 1906.

misled the Prussian Staff as to the practicability of concerted action.

Whether the Duke would have made a stand at Quatre-Bras if he had been fully aware of the state of affairs is a matter difficult to judge, but it appears needless to refute the suggestion of Delbruck, that a deliberately false misrepresentation was made to Blücher. It is curious to note that at this early stage in the campaign the leaders of the three armies had each been badly served by their Staffs as to the positions and marching movements of their troops.

Concentration at Ligny Early on the morning of June 16, Zieten withdrew his rear-guard from Fleurus, and, passing to the north side of the Ligny stream, formed up his corps in the villages of St. Amand, Bry and Ligny. The time allowed for the troops of the remaining Prussian corps to march in from their widely extended cantonments was apparently underestimated. At noon, the four divisions of the 1st Corps (Zieten) were drawn up in battle formation, while behind them, in support, was mustering the 2nd Corps (Pirch I). Thielmann, with the 3rd Corps, was in process of taking up the left of the position from Sombreffe, to the south of Tongrinne. At the same hour, the 4th Corps of Bülow only reached Hannut, a distance of twenty-five miles from the battlefield. Instead of having the whole Prussian army in position on the morning of June 16, but three of the corps would be assembled in the afternoon, with the 4th Corps unable to afford them any support.[1]

---

[1] Gneisenau omitted to inform Bülow that hostilities were imminent, and the latter, after concentrating his troops at Liège—on June 15—deferred further movement till the 16th. Had he

The situation became serious. There was no news from Wellington, firing was heard in the direction of Quatre-Bras, and the cavalry reported that a large force of the enemy was on the march from Charleroi towards Fleurus. At 10.45 there arrived a report from Bruneck at Quatre-Bras, dated 6.30 a.m., stating that the outposts were engaged to the north of Frasnes, and that the Prince of Orange was of the opinion that the whole of the Dutch-Belgian troops, and the larger part of the English army, would be concentrated in three hours near Nivelles. The Reserve from Brussels had also started for Quatre-Bras.[1]

Negligence of Gneisenau

L. V. 298

At noon there arrived a dispatch from Müffling, dated 7 p.m. the previous evening, which stated that the reports from Zieten had been received, that Wellington was concentrating his troops which would march when the moon rose [2] on Nivelles. A hope was expressed that there would be a victory on *June* 17.

L. V. 288

At about the same time there came a letter from the Duke " on the heights behind Frasnes, 10.30 a.m.," which gave an erroneous idea of the situation of the English army, and terminated with the words : " I do not see any large force of the enemy

App. 8

---

been made aware of the situation he could have effected his concentration towards Hannut on the 15th, and appeared on the battlefield the next day. A forcible example of the importance of explaining the situation and the objective of a movement in an operation order. The strained relations between Bulow and Gneisenau are discussed by Pflugk-Harttung, 252.

[1] It apparently took four hours for this dispatch to arrive from a position eight miles distant.

[2] The moon rose at midday on the 15th !

in front of us, and I await news from Your Highness, and the arrival of troops, in order to determine my operations for the day." The statement that Wellington designedly gave false details as to the position of the troops has been often confuted.[1]

Müffling did not learn of the proposed concentration of the Prussian army at Sombreffe till 9 p.m. on June 15, and in his dispatch (previously written) hopes for a successful battle on *June* 17. The Prussian Head Quarters Staff were fully aware of the extension of the Anglo-Dutch cantonments, and yet did not allow them time to effect a concentration.

Had Gneisenau forwarded the news that his troops were ordered at 12 p.m. on June 14 to concentrate at Sombreffe, Wellington would have grasped the situation in the early morning of the 15th, and given his orders accordingly.

It was quite natural that Gneisenau should expect assistance from Wellington, and that the Duke expected to be able to give it is evidenced by his riding out to meet Blücher. It was not a question of willingness, but one of opportunity. At one o'clock the two Marshals met in consultation on the heights of Bry, and, from the vantage of a mill, could see the French columns debouching on the plain below. "What do you want me to do?" said Wellington abruptly. A discussion, in which both Müffling and Gneisenau took part, continued for some time, and was finally closed by the Duke saying, "Well, I will come, provided I am not attacked myself." The manner in which the position

[1] The subject is discussed in detail by Pflugk-Harttung, pp. 232-52.

was occupied did not meet with Wellington's approval,[1] and, without giving any more formal engagement, he returned to Quatre-Bras to find how grossly he had been deceived by his Staff as to the concentration of his own forces.

[1] "If they fight here they will be damnably mauled," he said to Sir H. Hardinge (R. 155).

THE BATTLE OF QUATRE-BRAS

CHAPTER VIII

THE BATTLE OF QUATRE-BRAS

The Battlefield—Occupation of Position—The French Advance—Arrival of Jerome's Division—Charge of Van Merlen's Brigade—Arrival of Picton's Division—Second French Attack—Attack on Brunswick Corps—Charge and Repulse of Piré's Cavalry—Cannonade by Artillery—Cavalry Attack on Picton—Arrival of Alten's Brigades—Soult's Order of 3.15 p.m.—Charge of Cuirassiers—Advance of Foy—Attack on Right by Jerome—Attack on Left by Bachelu—Last Attack of Piré—Arrival of the Guards—The British Advance.[1]

The Battlefield

ON the cross-roads at the north-west corner of the Fleurus triangle stood a cluster of farm buildings that formed the hamlet of Quatre-Bras. Half a mile to the south the plain dipped to a rivulet running eastward to the Dyle, and then rose and fell in successive undulations towards Frasnes. The massive buildings of the Gemioncourt farm lay in a valley some 200 yards wide, which was bordered by hedges impassable for mounted troops, and presenting a formidable obstacle to the movement of infantry. To the westward the wood of Bossu, though of close growth in its interior, was sufficiently open on its outskirts to allow of cavalry and artillery passing through

---

[1] An analysis of many conflicting accounts has enabled me to place, for I believe the first time, in proper sequence the various phases of an action of a necessarily confused character.

it. An entry to the wood from the southward could be prevented as long as the Pierrepont farm was held. On the eastern flank the wood of La Hutte stretched from Frasnes up to the Namur road, while the village of Piraumont afforded a strong advanced post. With the further exception of an isolated farm and garden 250 yards south of Quatre-Bras the ground was open, but covered with rye standing as high as a man's shoulder.

Occupation of Position — In the forenoon of the 16th, the outposts extended from the Bois de Bossu to the Bois de la Hutte, and a desultory skirmishing between advanced troops foreshadowed a French advance. On his arrival from Brussels, Wellington rode to the outpost line, and before leaving (to interview Blücher), warned the Prince of Orange to hold his ground until reinforcements arrived.

For the defence, at the commencement of the battle, there were present nine battalions [1] of Perponcher's Dutch-Belgian division, with sixteen guns and some fifty cavalry—a total force of 7,000 men. To effectively occupy the position was impossible, but the cover afforded by the thickets and growing crops favoured a disposition of troops that would temporarily impose upon the enemy and delay his advance. Three battalions, with two guns, were placed on the right to hold Pierrepont farm and the wood of Bossu. The centre on both sides of the chaussée, with a support at Gemioncourt, was held by eleven guns, two battalions and a company, while on the left at Piraumont were formed the remaining companies of the Jager battalion.

L. V. 351

---

[1] The 7th Belgian Line Regiment did not arrive on the ground till 3.30 p.m., when it took post in the north of the Bossu wood.

THE BATTLE OF QUATRE-BRAS   83

The three remaining battalions, with three guns, were in reserve near Quatre-Bras.

The French Advance At 2.15 p.m. the French advanced to the attack in columns of brigades covered by skirmishers. The division of Foy moved on both sides of the main road, while that of Bachelu massed on their right, The 1st Chasseur Regiment of Piré flanked the right of Bachelu's troops, while the ancer brigade, with the 6th Chasseurs, was posted in rear of the interval between the two divisions. The attacking force numbered some 9,000 infantry, 1,850 cavalry, and twenty-two guns, but there was besides a reserve near Frasnes of 2,000 cavalry of the Guard, two batteries of artillery, and a brigade of Kellermann's cuirassiers.

The brunt of the attack fell upon the centre and left of the Allied line. The Jager companies, on the left, attacked by Bachelu and charged by Piré's chasseurs, fled in disorder from Piraumont. Foy, in overwhelming force, drove in the infantry and artillery holding the ground near the chaussée, and formed up his guns on the ridge originally held by the Allied forces. Two of the defending guns were captured, and the remainder retired half way to the crossroads.

L. V. 392

To stem the advance, the Prince of Orange led a counter attack on the artillery position, but charged by cavalry, and followed up by a brigade led by Foy in person, the Dutch battalions had to fall back to the northern edge of the ravine, leaving Gemioncourt in the hands of the enemy. The reserve battalions were meantime forwarded in support from Quatre-Bras.

Arrival of Jerome's Division

Jerome Bonaparte's division, some 8,000 strong, now appeared on the battlefield, and proceeded to attack the farm of Pierrepont, and the southern extremity of the Bossu wood. The French were everywhere pressing forwards, and the capture of Quartre-Bras seemed imminent. At this moment (a little before three o'clock) the head of Van Merlen's cavalry brigade was seen to be arriving from Nivelles and forming up to the east of the wood.

Charge of Van Merlen's Brigade

The two regiments had just completed a long forced march, and were in little condition for fighting, but the Prince ordered them to at once charge the skirmishers, that preceded the columns of Foy, that were advancing along the chaussée. The hussar regiment, *en fourrageur*, supported by the dragoons, made a gallant advance, but were checked by a heavy artillery fire, and charged in flank by the 6th Chasseurs and 5th Lancers. In the *mêlée* that ensued the French veterans gained the advantage and swept in vigorous pursuit close up to the crossroads. Here they were arrested at 3 p.m. by the sight

Arrival of Picton's Division

of the red-coats of the newly arrived troops of Picton, and, turning off to their right towards Gemioncourt, rode down a battalion of Dutch militia and disabled eight guns.

Perponcher's division was still holding its ground in the Bossu wood, but the French had cleared the approaches to Quatre-Bras, and the defence of the open plateau had to be undertaken by the on-coming reinforcements. Wellington had early realized the importance of holding Gemioncourt, and, on the arrival of the British infantry, sent forward a battalion to occupy it. It was too late, and the British brigades of Picton's division were at once deployed to the eastward, some little distance in front of the chaussée to Namur. The Hanoverian brigade formed in support to the north of the road, while the 95th Regiment secured a wood on the left flank opposite Piraumont. The corps of the Duke of Brunswick, which was following closely on Picton's troops, was at first placed in reserve, but one of its battalions was detached in support of the Allied left flank.

The movements of the British troops were carried out under a heavy fire from the French batteries, and there was every indication that the enemy were contemplating an attack in force. The Brunswick corps was then ordered to advance, and occupy the ground between the Brussels chaussée and the wood of Bossu.

It was now nearly four o'clock, and to withstand the attack of Reille's divisions and Piré's cavalry division, there was an Allied force standing on the defensive which (after making due allowances) was somewhat superior in infantry, but much weaker in cavalry and artillery.

Second French Attack, 4 p.m.
H. 201

As soon as Soult's order of 2 p.m. arrived from Fleurus, Ney, apparently for the first time, fully grasped the importance of the possession of Quatre-Bras, and ordered a general advance. The division of Bachelu descended into the valley of the stream, and, in crossing the hedges that bounded it, was broken up into small columns. Driving back the skirmishers, the French advanced over the plateau in close order till the heads of the columns came suddenly on the British line which had been moved forward into the high corn. Received by a terrific fire, the columns halted and recoiled, and Picton, without hesitation, ordered Kempt's brigade to advance at the charge.

Driving all before them, the English reached the edge of the valley, and poured a destructive fire on the flying enemy. The regiment on the left (79th), in its ardour, crossed the stream, but decimated by fire from the French artillery and supports, and charged by cavalry, it had to retire, and with the rest of the brigade return to its former position.

Attack on Brunswick Corps Further to the west the columns of Foy, with a brigade detached from Jerome, moved on both sides of the chaussée against the Brunswick corps, while the remainder of Jerome's division drove back the Dutch-Belgians in the wood.

The Brunswick skirmishers were giving way when the Duke charged with his lancers, in an endeavour to check the French advance. The veterans of Foy received the young troopers with a steady fire, and the advance of Piré's cavalry turned a check into a rout.

Charge and Repulse of Piré The French chasseurs, followed by lancers, galloped in vigorous pursuit, and, after dispersing the supporting infantry, pushed on to the cross-roads. The 6th Chasseur Regiment dashed in amongst the houses, and the Field-Marshal had a narrow escape from being cut down. Heavy loss was experienced from the fire of the 92nd Highlanders and the Nassau contingent, which had just arrived from Brussels, and but few of the gallant horsemen were able to again reform. The lancer brigade, following in support, finding they had gained the rear of the British line, wheeled about and charged the 42nd and 44th Regiments, which were on its right. The 42nd were caught in the act of forming square, and suffered severely; while the 44th, by order of their colonel, simply faced about, and successfully sustained the charge in line. The lancers thus repulsed galloped round the battalion, and eventually gained the bridge on the main road, while Wellington pushed forward two Brunswick battalions to their former position on the ground between the chaussée and the wood.

Cannonade by Artillery A heavy artillery fire was now directed for some time on the whole British front, and its cessation denoted a further attempt of cavalry to break the British squares. Ney was anxiously awaiting the arrival of D'Erlon with the 1st Corps before resuming the infantry attack. While Jerome was pushing forward in the wood, and Bachelu was pressing with his light troops on the Allied left, the combat in the centre was confined to artillery fire and the action of cavalry.

Cavalry Attack on Picton At about five o'clock Piré collected the whole of his available squadrons, and, moving from the west of Gemioncourt, made a further attempt to break the English squares. To relieve the 42nd and 44th Regiments in their exposed positions on the right of the line, Picton moved forward the united Royals and 28th Regiment, and directed the other regiments to adopt an échélon formation in columns of battalions. As the cavalry charged, the columns formed squares, and gave mutual aid by fire from their flanking positions. Chasseurs and lancers galloped in and out through the squares, vainly seeking for a weak point. A Hanoverian landwehr battalion near the Namur road was cut to pieces, but with no further success the squadrons, depleted in numbers, retired once more to reform, and the cannonade from artillery recommenced.[1]

Arrival of Alten's Brigade It was nearly 5.30 when the British brigade of Halkett and the Hanoverian brigade of Kilmansegge, with two batteries, opportunely reached the field of action from Nivelles. Shortly afterwards a horse artillery battery of Cooke's division arrived. Wellington had now some 30,000 men, with forty-eight guns, to oppose to the three divisions of Reille's corps (now some 15,000 strong), with thirty-eight guns. Owing to the repulse of the Dutch-Belgian and Brunswick troops, the Allied cavalry and artillery, though numerically superior, were overmatched by the artillery of Reille and the cavalry of Piré, while Ney still had in hand, near Frasnes, the cavalry of the Guard, and one brigade of Kellermann's corps.

Halkett's brigade of four battalions was advanced between the main Brussels road and the wood, and now formed the right of the British line with the Brunswick battalions. The Nassau contingent was forwarded to the support of the Saxe-Weimar troops, a portion of whom still held their positions in the Bossu thickets. The brigade of Kilmansegge continued its march to the left of the Allied line, and secured it against the advance of Bachelu.

---

[1] Sibborne is evidently in error as to the presence of cuirassiers. The brigade of Kellermann only took part in one charge against Alten's division. It is possible that a few cuirassiers or dragoons may have accompanied Piré's division, but it is more probable that the occupants of the severely tested squares gave the credit of breastplates to the cloaked chasseurs.

Soult's Order of 3.15 p.m. App. 5

Ney, shortly after five o'clock, received the news of the defection of D'Erlon, and the unwelcome intelligence was followed by the receipt of the dispatch that Soult sent at 3.15 p.m. from Fleurus. "You must manœuvre at once to envelop the right of the enemy . . . his army is lost if you act vigorously. The fate of France is in your hands. Do not hesitate a moment to execute the movement the Emperor orders . . ." But it was now too late. Quatre-Bras was occupied in force; all the French troops had been engaged, and there was no reserve but the cavalry of Kellermann and of the Guard. Maddened with the thought of his lost opportunities, Ney ordered Kellermann to charge, and make a desperate effort to retrieve the situation. The brigade of cuirassiers, 800 strong, was formed in squadron columns, and as it passed Gemioncourt the gallop was ordered. "I used great haste, so as not to allow my men to shrink, or perceive the whole extent of the danger in front of them."

Charge of Cuirassiers, 6 p.m.

On the slope to the eastward of the wood stood the newly arrived redcoats of Halkett's brigade. The 69th Regiment, somewhat in front of the chaussée, was in line,[1] and a momentary glimpse over the tall rye of glinting breastplates was followed by the rending of their ranks and the capture of the colours. Sweeping up the gentle incline, the squadrons, one after another, broke on the steady bayonets of the supporting squares, and then, galloping on, cut down the gunners of a battery, and dispersed a Brunswick battalion. The depleted

---

[1] Due to an order given by the Prince of Orange. Sibborne, 4th ed., 178.

squadrons, with breathless horses, now arrived in a circle of fire. From the Bossu wood, the embankment of the Namur road, and the houses of Quatre-Bras, the bullets sped fast, while from the road two guns firing case spread death through the ranks. Kellermann fell under his charger, and the officers in vain tried to rally their squadrons. The cuirassiers were deaf to all commands, and in disorderly groups galloped to the rear, and their flight was not arrested till near Frasnes.

Advance of Foy

The charge of Kellermann's brigade was followed up by an advance of two batteries and two columns of Foy's infantry, which obtained partial cover in the *lisière* of the wood. Before the squares of Halkett could form line they were fired into by artillery at short range. Lloyd's battery came into action, but he withdrew with two of his guns disabled, and the infantry moved in more or less disorder to the edge of the wood. Boldly advancing, the French reached the detached farm, some 300 yards in front of Quatre-Bras. Here they were charged by the 92nd Highlanders, and driven back to the edge of the wood, along which they slowly retired.

Attack on Right by Jerome

While the above attack was taking place to the immediate south of Quatre-Bras, the battalions of Jerome, on the right, had driven the defenders of the wood on Hautain-le-Val and to the northward, and had almost reached the Nivelles road.

Attack on Left by Bachelu

Determined efforts were simultaneously made by Bachelu to turn the Allied left. The skirmishers had already gained the high road when the 95th and the Brunswick battalion, now supported by Kilmansegge's Hanoverian brigade, charged forward, and, after an obstinate contest, drove back the French troops on Piraumont.

Last Attack of Piré
The immediate support of Kellermann's charge was by some mischance neglected by Ney. No orders were given to Lhéretier's remaining brigade, nor to the cavalry of the Guard, and it was not till the cuirassiers were fully engaged that Piré, once more with his chasseurs and lancers, charged the centre of the Allied line. The squares of Picton's division stood firm as the cavalry wave broke on them, and surging onwards dashed against the newly arrived Hanoverian battalions in support. In vain did the chasseurs and lancers return again and again to the charge, till Piré, in despair, withdrew the remnants of his squadrons behind Gemioncourt.

Arrival of the Guards, 6.30 p.m.
Such was the general position of affairs at about 6.30 p.m. when the 1st Division of Guards, under Cooke, arrived from Nivelles, and the remainder of the Brunswick corps from Brussels. Wellington had now on the field a force (excluding losses) of nearly 37,000 men, with sixty-eight guns.[1] The three divisions of Reille's corps with Piré's cavalry and Kellermann's cuirassiers, which were engaged in the action, amounted (excluding losses) to 20,000 men with forty-four guns.

The British Advance
The great superiority in force of the Allied army now enabled it to advance with a certainty of success. The Guard brigades were thrown into the Bossu wood and, after a stubborn

---

[1] The Nassau contingent of Krause should be added to the numbers given by Sibborne.

contest that lasted an hour, drove the troops of Jerome beyond its southern edge. Halkett and Pack, supported by Brunswick and Nassau battalions, advanced right and left of the chaussée, driving back Foy in front of them, while Kempt's brigade and the Hanoverians forced Bachelu, after a severe struggle, to abandon Piraumont. A battery of Foy's artillery arrested the advance of the Guards from the southern edge of the wood, and some of the troops that had emerged were charged by Piré's lancers. It was the last effort. It was getting dusk, and Ney fell back in good order on the heights north of Frasnes, just as D'Erlon rode up to report his arrival on the field. The loss sustained by the command of Ney was some 4,300 men, while that of the Allied forces was slightly greater.

THE BATTLE OF LIGNY

CHAPTER IX

THE BATTLE OF LIGNY[1]

Position of Ligny—Occupation of Position—The French Advance—The Left Attack by Vandamme—Counter Attack by Steinmetz and Pirch II—Flank Attack by Tippelskirch—Action at St. Amand—Appearance of D'Erlon—Advance of Blücher—The Fighting at Ligny—The Right Attack of Grouchy—The Attack of the Imperial Guard—The Close of the Battle.

Position of Ligny

FROM the village of Fleurus a wide stretch of fields of ripening corn sloped with gentle decline to a broad ravine, beyond which the rising ground formed a low range of hills, spreading in a curve from Bry to Tongrinne. The front of the Prussian position was along the Ligny stream—a rivulet whose banks formed a continuous ditch of sufficient depth to be an obstacle to mounted troops. Bordering the stream were a number of villages and hamlets with surrounding plantations and hedges. The buildings were chiefly of stone, with thatched roofs, and comprised several farm-houses, with large courtyards admirably adapted for defence.

Occupation of Position

On the forenoon of June 16, the corps of Zieten was massed on the heights of Bry, with a few battalions in front line from La

[1] The attacks of Vandamme on the Prussian right and of Gérard on Ligny took place simultaneously, but in the narrative they are for the sake of clearness each described separately from end to finish.

Haye to Ligny. The cavalry of the corps, under Roder, was advanced across the stream towards Fleurus. As the corps of Pirch I arrived, it was posted in support of the 1st Corps, and occupied the ground from the Roman road to Sombreffe. Somewhat later, Thielmann posted one of his divisions on the Fleurus road and one at Tongrinne, and pushed detachments forward to the stream. The remainder of the 3rd Corps were in reserve to the north of Sombreffe and at Point-du-Jour. The villages in front line were carefully prepared for defence, and their occupants strongly reinforced before the attack was delivered. The guns were posted on the hill slopes behind the stream.

R. 152

The total force under Blücher's command (omitting Bülow's corps) was some 87,000 men, inclusive of 8,500 cavalry and 224 guns.

The French Advance

It was eleven o'clock when Napoleon arrived on the scene. From the mill at Fleurus the troops at Bry could be clearly seen, and there was some justification for the idea that but one army corps was in position. At the Emperor's disposal was the corps of Vandamme and the cavalry corps of Grouchy, with the Imperial Guard in second line. But Gérard was late, and it was not till one o'clock that the arrival of his corps enabled a preliminary deployment to be made on the Fleurus road. The height of the growing crops, and the undulations of the ground, apparently concealed from view the arrival of the 2nd and 3rd Prussian Corps, and the Emperor despatched to Ney a report, that he was about to attack a " corps of troops " at half-past two o'clock, and enjoining him to assist in surrounding them.

THE BATTLE OF LIGNY

The movement of Prussian guns into position, and of infantry to the villages, made it soon clear that not a corps, but an army, was prepared to dispute further progress.

Gérard was ordered to wheel forward his command for the attack of the village of Ligny, while Vandamme, with Girard's division (2nd Corps) in support, moved towards St. Amand and La Haye. On the right, Grouchy, with his cavalry, was to hold in check the troops on the eastern flank of the Prussian position.

The fields of tall rye made the movement slow, and it was not till nearly three o'clock that Roder's cavalry was driven back, the guns got into position, and the columns stood formed, awaiting the final order for attack.

H. 165 "It is possible that three hours hence the fate of the war may be decided," said Napoleon to Gérard. A second and more peremptory dispatch was sent to Ney (dated 3.15 p.m.), and included the words: "So do not hesitate for a moment to make the movement the Emperor has ordered, and march on the heights of Bry and St. Amand."

As Soult was sending this order, a report came in from Lobau (at Charleroi) that Ney was opposed by 20,000 men at Quatre-Bras. This exaggerated statement [1] possibly led the Emperor to think that Ney might hesitate to carry out his instructions, and was the cause that a pencilled note was sent to Frasnes a quarter of an hour later, to the effect that the corps of D'Erlon should be detached for the attack on St. Amand.

Chap. X, R. 154 The force that assembled at Fleurus, and that took part in the battle, numbered some

[1] When Janin, the Staff Officer of Lobau, left Frasnes there was only Perponcher's division on the ground (H. 166).

68,000 men, including 13,000 cavalry and 210 guns (exclusive of Lobau's corps in reserve).

Left Attack, 3-4 p.m. Towards three o'clock, the guns of a battery of the Guard near Fleurus gave the signal for attack, and a furious cannonade was opened on the whole front of the enemy's line. Vandamme, without waiting for the artillery fire to take effect, pushed forward Lefol's division on St. Amand in three columns, covered by skirmishers. The march through the ripening corn was slow, and the Prussian cannon-shot ploughed their way in the dense masses. On nearing the village, the infantry fire from the outposts caused a momentary check, but with great ardour the French soldiery dashed into the enclosures, and, after a desperate fight at close quarters, drove the three defending battalions beyond the brook.

Counter Attack by Steinmetz Further advance was checked by the fire of artillery and infantry from the northern slope that dominated the stream. Steinmetz, who had charge of the defence of St. Amand, now brought up all his reserve battalions, and, after some severe fighting, succeeded in regaining part of the village. Finding his flank threatened, Vandamme called up to his assistance a portion of Berthezène's division, and directed Girard to advance on Le Hameau and La Haye. The impetuous attack of Girard

4-5 p.m. carried all before it. La Haye was captured, and the Prussians driven out of St. Amand, but the heavy fire of the artillery checked any advance across the stream. The guns of Vandamme now came into action, and it was evident that the right of the Prussian main position was seriously menaced. Blücher, without hesitation, sent forward the division of Pirch II (of Zieten's corps) from Bry to La Haye, while from the 2nd Corps of Pirch I he despatched towards Wagnelée the whole of Jurgass' cavalry and Tippelskirch's division to act on the French flank. Formed in lines of battalion columns, the infantry of Pirch II carried the upper part of La Haye, but an energetic counter attack drove them back across the stream. Reinforced by his second line, Pirch II returned to the attack, and, after a desperate street fight in which Girard was killed, the Prussian troops were for a second time forced back over the stream.

Counter Attack by Pirch II.

While this sanguinary contest was taking place at La Haye, the powerful flanking force (thirty-six squadrons and nine battalions) at Wagnelée came upon the field. Two brigades of cavalry were formed up between La Haye and Wagnelée, ready to fall on Girard's flank, while the infantry and remaining brigade moved forward. Vandamme had provided for such a movement by posting one of Habert's brigades, a battery, and all his cavalry opposite Wagnelée, with skirmishers well concealed in the corn. The Prussian battalions, marching with insufficient precautions, were taken utterly by surprise when smitten by well-directed volleys from the concealed troops, and fell back in confusion. The cavalry were held in check by Domont's chasseurs, and took scarcely any part in the action.

Flank Attack by Tippelskirch

Further to the eastward, at St. Amand, Zieten had brought up his 12-pounder batteries, and with their aid Steinmetz held his ground against every attempt at a forward movement by Vandamme.

Action at St. Amand

5–5.30 p.m. The Prussian forces had been gradually accumulating on the west of the battlefield with a view of assuming the offensive against the French left. Blücher, descending from the heights of Bry, arrived at La Haye at the moment when the infantry were being expelled from it by the last effort of Girard. Encouraged by the presence of their favourite leader, the troops once more pushed forward, and Girard's division, now depleted in numbers, was gradually forced back from house to house and hedge to hedge, till it reached Le Hameau, when a definite stand was made. At half-past five, every man, horse and gun of Vandamme's corps was fully employed. The remnant of two divisions were holding St. Amand and Le Hameau with difficulty, while the third division and the cavalry were deployed in front of Wagnelée. At this critical moment, a mass of some 20,000 men were seen in the distance, and were reported to be a column of the enemy that were marching on Fleurus.[1]

Appearance of D'Erlon

The news reached Napoleon at Fleurus at the moment when he was assembling the Guard for attack on Ligny. The movement was arrested, while he sent one of his Staff to reconnoitre the supposed enemy. To the assistance of Vandamme, whose troops were wavering, was at once despatched a division of the Young Guard, three regiments of the Old Guard, and the lancers

---

[1] There seems to have been no proper steps taken by Vandamme to find out the truth before reporting to Napoleon, and yet he had a cavalry division on his flank, and D'Erlon's advance was presumably headed by cavalry. The utter lack of initiative shown by cavalry in this campaign is once more in evidence.

of Subervie's division (from the extreme right of Grouchy).

6-7.30 p.m. At about six o'clock, a heavy cannonade preluded a formidable attack by Jurgass from Wagnelée against Le Hameau, while Pirch II, supported by fresh battalions from the 2nd Prussian Corps, assaulted St. Amand in three columns. The French now gave way at all points, but the newly arriving reinforcements, pressing forward with eager step, speedily recovered the lost ground; and, after heavy fighting, the French were again masters of St. Amand, and the nearest houses of La Haye.

Advance of Blücher Blücher was now aware that he could hope for no assistance from Wellington, but clung to the idea that he could still force back the French left on Fleurus. Reforming the exhausted battalions of the divisions of Pirch II, Brause and Tippelskirch, and calling up his last reserves, he led in person the attack once more. Le Hameau was again retaken, but the ranks dashed in vain against the steady formation of the Chasseurs of the Old Guard, and the Prussians retired in great disorder on La Haye. It was half-past seven, and the lowering clouds portended a storm of rain, when a furious cannonade was heard in the direction of Ligny.

During the whole time that the contest on the Prussian right was taking place, there was simultaneously a series of attacks being made on the village of Ligny.

Repeated Attack on Ligny, 3.15-7.30 Gérard's corps was weak in numbers, and one of his divisions was handed over to support Grouchy's attack on the left of the Prussian position. There were, therefore, but two divisions of infantry, some 10,000 strong, to capture a village prepared for defence and held by some 9,000 men. Ligny consisted mainly of two streets, one north and one south of the stream, while the church, and cemetery, the farms and the chateau were admirably adapted for defence. Pécheux's division advancing in three columns were thrice repulsed, but a fourth effort enabled the French to hold the houses south of the stream. When occasion offered, the guns of both sides shelled the houses, the roofs took fire, and the battle at this point was confined to a desperate village fight. Gérard had to push in his last reserves, while the exhausted defenders were from time to time reinforced by fresh battalions. Prussians and French crossed and recrossed the brook in turns, and the fury of the struggle continued till the close of the battle with unabated force.[1]

Right Attack of Grouchy On the right of the French army, Grouchy, with his cavalry and only one infantry division of Gérard, could do little more than occupy the attention of Thielmann's corps. The outlying villages of Boignée and Balatre were summarily taken, and, with the help of the infantry, the line of the brook was afterwards carried at Tongrenelle and Potriaux.

It was not till half-past six o'clock that the Emperor at Fleurus learnt that the hostile column, reported by Vandamme, was really the 1st Corps of D'Erlon. The aide-de-camp who had been sent to reconnoitre did no more than satisfy himself as to the composition of the column, and there is no evidence to show that he

---

[1] It is worth while to read the description of the fight in the *Waterloo* of Erckmann-Chatrain.

brought intelligence of the recall of the 1st Corps to Quatre-Bras.[1]

Here, in full view of the Prussians on the Bry heights, D'Erlon received the imperative order of Ney to return to Frasnes: "I decided," said he, "that as he summoned me back in direct opposition to Napoleon's will, the Marshal must be in extreme peril." No further orders were received from the Emperor, and D'Erlon, with three of his divisions, retraced his steps, and with troops "irritated and ashamed at having done nothing," reached Frasnes at nightfall. One division and the cavalry of the corps was left opposite Wagnelée, with a caution "to be prudent." Jacquinot's cavalry skirmished with those of the enemy that covered the Prussian right flank, while Durutte ousted a feeble rear-guard from Wagnelée. Paralysed by D'Erlon's instructions as to prudence, he here allowed the enemy to defile from Le Hameau and La Haye to the heights of Bry within easy range of his guns. Time was pressing, and light was failing when Napoleon resumed the suspended movement of the Guard, and led them personally to the attack.

H. 219

Attack of the Guard, 7.30 p.m.

The batteries of the reserve came into action against the Ligny heights, while the Old Guard advanced in two columns against the east and west of the village. Following the infantry were the cuirassiers of Milhaud on the

---

[1] The fact that a single junior officer was sent to reconnoitre a presumably hostile column seems almost incredible. Clausewitz writes somewhat naturally of a troop of cavalry. Delcambre, sent by Ney, would probably have reached D'Erlon with his order of recall at about the same time that the Emperor's aide-de-camp arrived at the column.

right, while the Emperor led the cavalry of the Guard on the left flank. The troops of Gérard, exhausted by their past efforts, now gained heart, and the whole force, with a vigorous rush, pushed across the stream, and drove the defenders at the point of the bayonet out of the northern outskirts of Ligny.

The Guard, flanked by cavalry, had been driven like a wedge into the centre of the Prussian line. The 1st and 2nd Prussian Corps, weakened by the desperate struggle at La Haye and St. Amand, were on the right of the position; Thielemann, with two of his divisions, was being pressed by Grouchy on the left, while the reserves at Sombreffe were too distant to afford immediate support. To repel the attack there were only the fragments of the brigades that had fought at Ligny throughout the afternoon and the cavalry of Zieten's corps. The infantry were too shaken to offer much resistance to the serried columns of the Guard, and the only intact troops were the thirty-two squadrons of Roder's cavalry.

Blücher, galloping down from La Haye, now arrived on the scene, and, checking the retreat of the batteries and battalions, ordered the cavalry to attack. The successive charges of the Prussian cavalry regiments met with little success against the squares of the French Guard, and the formidable squadrons of cuirassiers and dragoons. His own charger was shot, and the gallant Marshal was with difficulty extricated from the *mêlée* of horsemen. Till nightfall the intermingled squadrons of French and Prussians surged backwards and forwards on the slopes of the hill, while the columns of the Guard pressed forward steadily to the heights of Bussy. The desperate charges of the Prussian cavalry covered the retreat of the artillery, and, though the infantry of the centre were put in disorderly flight, the troops on both flanks retired in good order.

At the close of the battle the corps of Zieten and Pirch were covered by a strong rear-guard at Bry, while Sombreffe and Point-du-Jour were occupied by Thielmann.

The corps of Lobau had followed up the French advance, and bivouacked in front line near the mill of Bussy, while the remaining French corps passed the night on the slopes which constituted the original Prussian position.

On the open ground, and in the villages lay some 12,000 Prussians and 8,500 French dead and wounded, while some twenty-seven guns fell into the hands of the victors.

THE D'ERLON EPISODE

CHAPTER X

THE D'ERLON EPISODE

The March of D'Erlon—The Change of Direction—What was the Order?—Who Gave the Order?—Who was Responsible?—The Effect of the Order—Misapprehension of Napoleon—Comments.

The March of D'Erlon

VARIOUS theories have been broached to account for the futile march of D'Erlon's corps between the two battlefields, and its inability to take part in the actions either of Ligny or Quatre-Bras. The presence of the corps with Ney would have enabled him to repulse the attack of Wellington, while, had it made a flank attack at Ligny, there is a strong probability that the Prussian defeat would have culminated in disaster. Had the 20,000 men of D'Erlon been utilized on either battlefield, the operations of the Allies would have developed on quite different lines, and the misunderstanding that so seriously prejudiced the cause of Napoleon requires a detailed explanation. For reasons that have already been stated, D'Erlon, on June 16, did not follow closely on the rear of Reille's corps, but delayed his advance from Gosselies till 3 p.m.

H. 205

The Change of Direction

At four o'clock the leading division of Durutte had crossed the Roman road on its march towards Frasnes.[1] A little later—

[1] The movements of D'Erlon had hitherto been slow. The

some time between 4 p.m. and 4.30 p.m.—galloped up a Staff officer from Napoleon and showed to Durutte a letter addressed to Ney (or D'Erlon), and directed him in accordance with its purport to divert the column by way of Villers Peruin on towards the battle taking place at Ligny.[1] It must have been about 4.30 p.m. that the head of D'Erlon's column left the main road, and in an hour's march it would be within sight of Vandamme, who was attacking St. Amand and La Haye. It seems probable that the rearmost troops were directed to move by the Roman road, and it is at all events certain from the report of Vandamme that the corps approached the Ligny battlefield in a formation sufficiently broad and dense as to enable to it be estimated at from 20,000 to 30,000 men.

It is a subject of interest to know : (1) What order was it that produced such a momentous decision ? (2) Who was responsible that it should be effectively carried out ? and (3) Why did a Staff officer take upon himself to forestall it ? The answers to these questions to a certain extent overlap, but they may, for the sake of clearness, be considered separately.

What was the Order ? App. 4

What order was it? From Fleurus in the afternoon there was despatched to Ney the 2 p.m. order of Soult. The Emperor intimated that he was about to attack "*un corps de troupes,*" and enjoined Ney to also attack what was in front of him, and afterwards combine

---

weather was sultry, and the rate of march would not exceed 2½ miles an hour for the leading troops.

[1] It is significant that Durutte obeyed the order without comment, while the same general, two hours later before Wagnelée, shirked his responsibilities.

with the Emperor in enveloping the Prussian corps. The order was sent by way of Gosselies, and reached Ney on the battlefield of Quatre-Bras at 4 p.m.[1] It is inconceivable that any Staff officer should have taken upon himself the responsibility of tampering with a preliminary order of this nature, and the bearer of it would have reached Gosselies just as the 1st Corps was marching out of it.[2] At 3.15 p.m., when the armies were fully engaged at Ligny, a second order was sent charging Ney to manœuvre so as to fall on the flank and rear of the Prussians: "Cette armée est perdue si vous agissez vigoureusement; le sort de la France est entre vos mains. Ainsi n'hésitez pas un instant pour faire le mouvement que l'Empereur vous ordonne." It seems probable that this despatch was conveyed by the same route as the previous one, as it took two hours to reach Ney. The bearer would catch up the leading divisions of D'Erlon about halfway between the Roman road and Frasnes, and the tenor of the order is so clear and insistent that one is able to conceive a Staff officer taking the unusual step of forestalling its provisions.

App. 5

There was, however, a third pencilled order issued at 3.30 p.m. of an even more imperative nature. It appears that after the despatch of the 3.15 p.m. order a report came from Lobau to the effect that Quatre-Bras was held by 20,000 men. The Emperor realized that Ney, if confronted by a large force, might hesitate to act on the 3.15 p.m. despatch. It was all-important to

[1] The distance is twelve miles by road, and the rate that messages were carried was approximately six miles an hour.

[2] The contention of Ropes that it was this order that was shown to Durutte seems unjustifiable (R. 182).

defeat the Prussian army, while it would be quite sufficient for the left wing simply to hold the English force and prevent it giving assistance to its ally. In haste, therefore, a quarter of an hour later, and by the direct road through Mellet, a pencilled note [1] was sent directing that at all events D'Erlon's corps must be at once despatched towards St. Amand. By the short cut taken the Roman road was but five miles distant, and the bearer of the despatch would overtake the leading division of D'Erlon shortly after it crossed the road. It seems probable that it was this pencilled order upon which the Staff officer acted when he took the responsibility of directing the troops of the 1st Corps towards the Ligny battlefield.

Who Gave the Order? *Why did the Staff officer divert the columns?* The usual explanation that an aide-de-camp, in excess of zeal, forestalled an order which he was carrying to a superior officer is scarcely sufficient. A study of the memorable four days makes it clear that even the senior officers of the French army were singularly dependent on Napoleon, and were averse to taking responsibility. To deliberately forestall an order given to a marshal (or a corps commander) implies that the officer thus acting would be one of high position who knew that his action would be approved of by the Emperor. Napoleon on the 17th expressed his displeasure at the measures taken by both Ney and

---

[1] The exact terms of this note are not known. It might have been a duplicate of the 3.15 p.m. order sent by a Staff officer, who was verbally made acquainted with the Emperor's views. The wording given by De Salle from memory is not convincing (H. 206). It at all events contained a direct reference to D'Erlon's corps being detached. See note p. 97

D'Erlon, but no mention is made of the officer who initiated the flank march of the 1st Corps towards Ligny. The name of the bearer of the pencilled note is of little importance. It was in all probability General Labadoyère, as D'Erlon made no objection to his action, nor did the Emperor subsequently blame him. Had an officer of inferior rank borne the message, it would imply that he had the direct authority of the Emperor for the course he took.[1]

Who was Responsible?
App. 9

Who was responsible for the movement? It is clear that Napoleon intended D'Erlon to move towards Ligny. "Si le comte d'Erlon avait executé le mouvement sur St. Amand que l'Empereur a ordonné, l'armée Prussienne etait totalement détruite."[2] Whether Ney or D'Erlon was in fault as to the manner in which the movement was carried out is a matter of dispute.

H. 206
G. 93

To whom was the pencilled order addressed? Houssaye has collected a number of statements favouring the view that a direct order was issued to D'Erlon while Grouard, in a lengthy and able disquisition, points out that this is improbable.

---

[1] The publication of his letters in the *Matin* of March, 1899, makes it clear that Forbin-Janson did not carry this message. It is possible that Colonel Laurent, *par la volonté positive de Napoléon,"* was responsible for the movement (G. 80). In an old narrative by Picton (1816) it is stated that Labadoyère (the Adonis of Paris) was in Brussels on the night of the 15th, and in the garb of a Belgian officer shook hands with the Duke. If there is any truth in this, it shows the General to be of a singularly energetic and daring character.

[2] "Le comte d'Erlon a eu de fausses directions, car s'il eut executé l'ordre de mouvement que l'Empereur avait proscrit, l'Armée Prussienne etait totalement détruite" (Soult a Davout, June 17).

App. 6

H. 211

App. 9

App. 16

The recently discovered letter of Ney of June 16 is good evidence, and states: "Un malentendu de la part du Comte d'Erlon m'a privé de l'espèrance d'une belle victoire." This clearly implies that a direct order was not sent by the Emperor to D'Erlon, and that the latter had no business to divert his march without the Marshal's consent. This view is also supported by the fact that as soon as Ney heard of D Erlon's movement he at once sent an order of recall. On the morning of the 17th the Emperor complains that Ney did not keep the corps of D'Erlon and Reille united, before he makes any mention of D'Erlon not having executed the movement that had been ordered. But if Napoleon expected the two corps to be united for the attack on Quatre-Bras, any order sent for the detachment of one of the corps would necessarily be addressed to the Marshal commanding the whole force.

The Emperor himself never admitted that he had sent a direct order to D'Erlon, and states that the march of the 1st Corps is difficult to explain. D'Erlon states that he was riding ahead of his corps when Labadoyère showed him the pencilled order addressed to Ney, and explained to him that he had already diverted the corps in accordance with its tenor.[1] He also points out that if the order of the Emperor had been issued to him directly, it would have been punctually executed, and there would have been no question of

---

[1] The letter of Ney to the Duke of Otranto (June 26, 1815) is inconsistent with his despatch of June 16, and the statements in it must be received with hesitation. Ney was on his defence, and was striving to throw all the blame of failure in the campaign on the shoulders of Napoleon.

a counter-march from Ligny to Quatre-Bras. The above explanation is the only one that tallies with the events as they actually occurred. Ney, in striving to exculpate himself, states that the Emperor sent back to him the corps of D'Erlon from Ligny, and ignores his own pressing order to Delcambre. But the fact that Ney issued an order for recall is testified to by many witnesses. The outcome was most disastrous. As the corps of D'Erlon approached the battlefield of Ligny it was reported to be a hostile column, and before the truth was realized the advance of the Guard was checked for more than an hour.[1] The return of the corps towards Quatre-Bras was a fatal error due to D Erlon. "I thought that since the Marshal had taken upon himself to recall me, it was a matter of urgency." To go forward might have momentous results, while to retire meant not reaching Ney till darkness fell. It was one of those cases where "intelligent disobedience" such as that of Perponcher the same morning would have been amply justified.

Charras, 199

The Effect of the Order

App. 16

Misappresion of Napoleon

The astonishment of Napoleon on seeing at 5.30 p.m. a column advancing towards him from Quatre-Bras is capable of explanation. He had every reason to suppose that the order sent for the detachment of D'Erlon would have reached Ney when the corps was in support near Frasnes. If the Emperor's instructions of the morning of the 16th had been carried out, one division would also be near

---

[1] The staff officer sent by Napoleon to reconnoitre the column returned to him about 6.30 p.m. (H. 181).

Marbais. The order of 3.15 p.m. or the pencilled order could certainly not be acted on till at least five o clock, and if promptly carried out would result in the divisions of the 1st Corps being seen at six o'clock moving in the direction of Bry by the Namur chaussée or to the south of it. Instead of this, at 5.30 p.m. a column is reported to be marching directly on Fleurus! The possibility of D'Erlon not having followed on the rear of Reille's corps was not allowed for, and apparently the diversion of his march by Labadoyère was not communicated to him.[1]

There is reason to suppose that a verbal order to attack at once was afterwards sent to D'Erlon by the Emperor, and reached Durutte's division, but the General shirked the responsibility of carrying it out, and referred it to his corps commander, who was already on his retreat westwards.

In respect of the whole D'Erlon episode, it would seem that Ney under the circumstances can only be blamed for his hasty order of recall. D'Erlon showed remissness in not informing the Marshal sooner of the change of direction of his corps, and committed a grave error in counter-marching at an hour when such a movement could be of no use, while Napoleon, as was often his wont, trusted too much to the judgment of his subordinate generals, and did not give his directions in sufficient detail or with the necessary precision.

[1] Houssaye lays stress on a misunderstanding by D'Erlon of the terms of the pencilled order, while Lettow Vorbeck attaches more importance to the data of time and space (H. 209; L. V. 332).

THE MORNING OF THE 17TH JUNE—
NAPOLEON

CHAPTER XI

THE MORNING OF THE 17TH OF JUNE—NAPOLEON

Napoleon at Fleurus—Orders to Ney—Ride to Ligny—Advance on Marbais—Orders to Grouchy.

Napoleon at Fleurus

THROUGHOUT the whole of June 16 the Emperor was left in ignorance of what was taking place at Quatre-Bras, and the firm attitude displayed by the Prussian troops at Bry and Sombreffe precluded all idea of a pursuit by night. The outposts of the two armies were in close contact, and the French bivouacked on the field of battle, with a portion of their troops under arms. Napoleon rode back to Fleurus and gave orders [1] to Grouchy to pursue the enemy at daybreak towards Gembloux and Namur with the cavalry of Pajol and Exelmans. At midnight a despatch was received from Ney stating that a severe action had been fought, and deploring that the mistake made by D'Erlon deprived him of a brilliant victory. Soult, on the other hand, apparently took no measures to inform Ney as to the result of the battle of Ligny,

H. 225

App. 6

---

[1] Jomini states that orders were also issued to move on Tilly and to the northward; but at all events they were not carried out. From the Grouchy *Memoirs* it would seem that the Marshal issued orders to his cavalry without any instructions from the Emperor (G. 265).

though Frasnes, by the direct road, was less than eight miles from Fleurus.

On the morning of June 17, towards seven o clock, Flahault returned from Frasnes with an account of the battle of Quatre-Bras, while about the same time a report arrived from Pajol that he was pursuing the enemy on the Namur road, and had made many prisoners. Grouchy came for orders, but was told to wait and accompany the Emperor to the battlefield, where he proposed to inspect the troops. A long despatch was sent to Ney at 8 a.m., commenting on the fact that he had not kept his command united, and that D'Erlon had not executed the movement ordered. He was informed that the Prussian army had been routed, and that if there was only a rear-guard at Quatre-Bras, he should attack it and occupy the position. In the event of the English being in force, the Emperor would march on their flank from Bry, while Ney attacked their front. The despatch terminated with the statement that the day would be needed to terminate this operation and in re-victualling the army, supplying ammunition, and caring for the wounded. Napoleon was rightly of opinion that Wellington, on hearing of the defeat of Blücher, would retire towards Brussels under cover of a rear-guard.

Orders to Ney App. 9 R. 384

Before starting for Ligny an order was sent to Lobau to despatch Teste's division, with its battery, to the support of Pajol, while a cavalry reconnaissance was made towards Quatre-Bras.

Ride to Ligny

The Emperor and his Staff, about 9 a.m., set out for the battlefield, and after visiting Ligny, St. Amand and the vicinity of La Haye, arrived on the Bussy heights. So great was the cheering with which he was received by the troops that the sound was heard by the Prussian cavalry at Tilly.

<small>H. 229</small>

Every moment was now of value. The real direction of the Prussian retreat was not known, and no attempt had been made to follow up the enemy's right wing or to reconnoitre to find out the course it had taken. More than six hours of daylight had gone, and the Emperor, with inexplicable lethargy, let the minutes pass in discussing with his generals the politics of Paris and other irrelevant subjects. "The Napoleon we have known no longer lives," said Vandamme. "Our success of yesterday will have no results."

Between ten and eleven o'clock a despatch (dated 6.30 a.m.) was received from Ney, giving an estimate of the English forces at Quatre-Bras, while the reconnoitring party which had been sent westward returned with the news that they had been driven back by British cavalry. From the other flank Pajol reported that, at Le Mazy on the Namur road, he had captured a battery and numerous wagons, and it was known that Exelmans' dragoons had marched on Gembloux.

Advance on Marbais
<small>H. 232</small>

It was now about eleven o'clock, and the Emperor ordered Lobau to take his corps to Marbais, with the intention of supporting the attack of Ney on Quatre-Bras. Drouot, with the Imperial Guard, was to follow in support. Subsequently, the cavalry division of Domon of Vandamme's corps, and that of Subervie, with the cuirassiers of Milhaud, from Grouchy's command, were ordered in the same direction.

Orders to Grouchy

Verbal instructions were given to Grouchy to follow up the Prussian retreat. The purport of these instructions was disputed for many years, but the matter was cleared up by the coming to light, in 1842, of an order to Grouchy, dictated by the Emperor to General Bertrand (in the absence of Soult), and issued some little time before noon on June 17. The general purport of the despatch was:

App. 11

"Concentrate on Gembloux, reconnoitre towards Namur and Maestricht. Pursue the enemy, and inform me of his movements. It is of importance to know what the enemy is intending to do—whether they are separating from the English, or *whether they intend still to unite, and risk the fate of another battle.* Occupy every evening a good military position, with several avenues of retreat. Post detachments of cavalry so as to communicate with me by the chaussée of Namur."

R. 210

Napoleon had now arranged for the pursuit of Blücher, and on Soult's arrival at noon sent a peremptory order to Ney to attack the enemy at Quatre-Bras, and informed him that he would be supported by the troops now at Marbais. The Emperor then mounted his horse, and rode along the chaussée to the head of his troops. The retreat of the English army to Waterloo was now followed up by Napoleon, while the Prussians moving on Wavre were pursued by Grouchy.

THE ENGLISH RETREAT

CHAPTER XII

THE ENGLISH RETREAT

Wellington at Genappe—Decision to Retire—Retreat on Genappe—Advance of French Army—The Pursuit—Action at Genappe—Napoleon at Belle Alliance—The Military Situation—Orders for Battle.

Wellington at Genappe

WELLINGTON slept at Genappe on the night of June 16, and rode out to Quatre-Bras in the early morning. The bulk of the cavalry from Ninhove under Lord Uxbridge had arrived, while the brigade of Ompteda, the divisions of Clinton and Colville, and the reserve of artillery were moving at daybreak on Quatre-Bras and Nivelles.

Müffling had kept Blücher informed of the progress of the fighting at Quatre-Bras on the 16th, and at 8 p.m. a report arrived from the field of Ligny that the

H. 259

Prussian Field-Marshal was assuming the offensive, and that "all was well." No further intelligence arrived during the night,[1] and the impression was left that the action would be resumed all along the line on the following morning. From Staff officers sent out both by Wellington and Müffling definite news at last arrived about 7.30 a.m. that the Prussian army had been defeated and had retired on Wavre.

[1] A despatch from Gneisenau as to the defeat at Ligny conveyed by Major Winterfeldt was delayed owing to his being wounded and thrown from his horse (H. 259; Chesney, 161).

Decision to Retire

R. 386

It was impossible to remain longer at Quatre-Bras and be exposed to the combined attack of Napoleon and Ney. "Old Blücher has had a d——d good licking and gone back to Wavre, eighteen miles. As he has gone back, we must go back too."

There were no signs of activity on the part of the enemy in the direction of Frasnes, and the retreat did not commence till 10 a.m. on June 17. But orders had been previously issued for the troops at Nivelles to start at the same hour for Waterloo by the Braine l'Alleud road, for the brigades at Braine-le-Comte to halt, and for the forces at Enghien to move towards Hal.

The delay of some two hours in retreating might have led to a dangerous situation if the French forces had advanced in the early morning, but the risk was taken, not so much for the convenience of the troops at Quatre-Bras, as to ensure a simultaneous retreat from Nivelles. To the last the Duke seemed apprehensive of a turning movement by Hal.

At about 9 a.m. a Prussian Staff officer, Lieutenant von Massow,[1] arrived from Mellèry with a verbal report to Müffling as to the intended concentration at Wavre, and to inquire what the Duke proposed to do. In answer to this Wellington stated that he was falling back on Mont St. Jean, and would give battle if the Field-Marshal would support him even with a single corps.[2] Otherwise he would be compelled to sacrifice Brussels and retire behind the Scheldt.

H. 261

---

[1] Von Massow on his return reached Wavre at noon.
[2] According to Gneisenau two corps were asked for (L. V. 527; Müffling's History [Sinclair], 16).

THE ENGLISH RETREAT

Retreat on Genappe — At the hour appointed (10 a.m.) the divisions of Cooke and Picton, followed by the troops of Perponcher and Brunswick, filed in succession up the Brussels road, while Alten's division, reinforced by some Brunswick battalions, covered the retirement. Ompteda's brigade was first withdrawn to Sart-Dame-Avelines and the woods of Les Censes, while Halkett's and Kilmansegge's brigades retired to a second and third position further north.

Sib. 265 — The outpost troops from the south of the wood of Bossu to the Namur road fell back slowly on Ompteda's brigade, while cavalry piquets gradually replaced them from Uxbridge's cavalry, which was drawn up in two lines in front of the chaussée. The whole of Alten's division, retiring by successive brigades, crossed the Genappe stream by way of Bézy and the bridge of Wais-le-Hutte. The hussars of Vivian protected the movement from any advance from the direction of Namur.

Orders had been given for the heavy cavalry to retire by the main Brussels road, covered by the 23rd Light Dragoons and the 7th Hussars. Vandeleur's and Vivian's brigades were to cross the Genappe stream by the bridge at Thuy, while the dragoons of the King's German Legion passed by a ford above the village of Genappe.

Sib. 271

Advance of French Army — Such were the general dispositions about noon, when a formidable French force consisting of the corps of Lobau, the Imperial Guard, and the cavalry divisions of Subervie, Domon, Jacquinot and Milhaud were forming up on the Namur road. From Bry the Emperor (at noon) had sent a definite order to Ney to attack

H. 239

the Quatre-Bras position, and report progress to Marbais, from whence an advance in co-operation would be made.

<small>App. 10</small>

At one o'clock Napoleon took command of his troops, and, hearing nothing from Frasnes, determined to push forward. The hussars of Marbot had fallen back before the English vedettes, and were detached towards Ney to further his immediate advance. The main body was formed up in order of battle, and the front line, consisting of mounted artillery flanked by cavalry, pushed forward at a trot. The Emperor himself with his service squadrons galloped on in advance.

<small>The Pursuit, 2 p.m.</small>

The sky was overcast with clouds and a high wind portended a storm, when from Quatre-Bras were seen the masses of French cavalry on the Namur road and the columns of D'Erlon's infantry advancing from the south. It was time for the English rear-guard to retire. As the piquets galloped in the guns opened fire on the pursuing squadrons, and the hussar brigade fell back in line covered by the patrols of Vandeleur's brigade. Mercer's battery had only time to fire one salvo before limbering up. "The report was instantly followed by an awful clap of thunder and lightning that almost blinded us. The rain came down as if a waterspout had broken over us. . . . As if in mockery of the elements the French guns still sent forth their feebler glare, and now scarcely audible reports, their cavalry darting on at a headlong pace, adding their shouts to the uproar."

<small>Mercer, 1, 270</small>

Neither the centre nor the right column were harassed in their retreat while on the south

<small>Sib. 273</small>

side of the Genappe stream. Vivian's brigade, however, in its movement on Thuy was hotly pursued in the blinding rain, and his guns with difficulty escaped capture. Checked at the bridge by the fire of dismounted men, and hampered by the rain-sodden soil, the French cavalry gave up the pursuit and moved towards the Charleroi-Brussels road. The main body of the English cavalry, after passing through the village of Genappe, formed up with its artillery in two lines on the rising ground beyond. Through the winding street of the village were advancing the strong cavalry force which now formed the advanced guard of the Imperial army. As the French lancers debouched from the northern exit they were charged with indifferent success by the 7th Hussars. Lord Uxbridge then sent forward two squadrons of the Life Guards, who, riding down their lighter opponents, drove them back into the centre of the village. The check was a temporary one, and Napoleon in person, with a horse artillery battery of the Guard and his service squadrons endeavoured to put vigour in the pursuit. The weather, however, was terrible. "It rained in such a way as I never saw either before or since: it seemed as if the water were tumbled out of tubs . . . the ground was so soft that at every step our horses sunk halfway to the knees." The movement of cavalry over open ground became more and more difficult, and it was impossible to turn the flanks of the retiring force. Covered by their light troops, the whole of Lord Uxbridge's command retired slowly with but little loss on Waterloo. It was half-past six when Napoleon at the head of

Action at Genappe

Max. I. 272

Napoleon at Belle Alliance H. 272

his cavalry reached La Belle Alliance. The rain had ceased, and through the mist loomed in the distance large masses of troops that evidently formed the main army of Wellington. A cannonade was kept up between a few batteries with but little effect till put a stop to by the dim light.

Napoleon rested for the night at the farm of "Le Caillou" some mile and a half in rear of La Belle Alliance. Towards 9 p.m. Milhaud informed him that his patrols had encountered Prussian cavalry at Tilly, and had followed them as far as Mont St. Guibert. It was stated that a despatch was thereupon sent to Grouchy directing him to march on St. Lambert as soon as he had ascertained that Blücher had evacuated Wavre, but it is somewhat doubtful if such a message was sent, and it is certain in any case that it never reached its destination.

H. 277

The Military Situation The situation was apparently not correctly appreciated at the French Head Quarters. It was thought that by the defeat at Ligny the Prussian army was so much demoralized that a small corps would be sufficient to watch it. At Blücher's heels was a force of 33,000 men, and even if the whole of his army retired on Wavre it would be held in check by Grouchy. A retreat of the Allied armies northwards for the purpose of concentrating in front of Brussels was the course most likely to be pursued, but that Blücher would risk a flank march towards Planchenoit or Ohain while (presumably) being hotly pursued seemed almost incredible. The main point was to prevent the junction of the English and Prussian forces, and to defeat Wellington

H. 279

before he could be assisted by an ally who would require some days to be in a condition to fight. There was a fear that the Duke would manage to slip away in the night through the Soignes forest, and were Blücher in a position to join him the situation from a French point of view was very serious. But all this was mere conjecture, as it was quite possible that the Prussians were retiring on Liège and the Rhine.

Wellington, on the other hand, had determined to give battle if the Prussians would send one or two of their corps to his assistance. There was no doubt that Blücher himself was willing to co-operate, but difficulties might arise from the conditions of the Prussian retreat or from the undisguised hostility of Gneisenau. The Duke had good reason to be anxious for the morrow,[1] but the confidence of his troops was not shaken by any preliminary arrangements for retreat. At last, in the early morning of June 18—before three o'clock—arrived the definite assurance that Bülow, supported by another corps, would move at daybreak on St. Lambert. The dispositions of the troops in line of battle had already been arranged, and nought remained but for Staff officers to lead them to their appointed places.

Order for Battle

Before retiring to rest the Emperor dictated an order of battle for the next day, but in a state of anxiety as to whether Wellington was still holding his ground, he made a round of the outposts at one o'clock in the morning. The rain

[1] The testimony that the Duke rode to Wavre on the night of the 17th to confer with Blücher proves on analysis to be untrustworthy. Roper, in his last edition, admits as conclusive the notes of Baron Gurney as to a conversation with Wellington on the subject. "I did not see Blücher the day before Waterloo" (R. 242).

was falling heavily, and complete silence prevailed. Through a veil of rain and smoke the innumerable camp fires in the distance still lit up the horizon, and there were no signs of a movement of retreat.

Returning to his quarters in the early dawn, he found the despatch of Grouchy written at Gembloux at 10 p.m. on the 17th. It distinctly stated that "if the bulk of the Prussians retire on Wavre, I shall follow them in that direction, in order that they may not be able to reach Brussels, and to separate them from Wellington." The tenor of the message was of a nature to strengthen Napoleon's views that a Prussian flank movement towards Wellington would be impracticable. Shortly afterwards the reports from the outposts, confirmed by Belgian deserters, made it clear that the English army was resolved to maintain its position.

R. 359
App. 12.

The enemy was now in his grasp, and victory to the Emperor seemed certain. He was anxious to attack as soon as possible, but the soil was so soaked with rain that the movements of guns would be difficult. Some few hours must be allowed for the sun to dry and partially harden the ground, and orders were given that the army should be formed up ready to attack at 9 a.m.

H. 286

THE PRUSSIAN RETREAT

CHAPTER XIII

The Prussian Retreat

The Night of Ligny—The Order for Retreat—The Movement on Wavre—Comments—The Movement in Detail—Messages between Allies—Decision to join Wellington—Orders for the March—The March to Waterloo—Defective Staff Arrangements.

The Night of Ligny

THE failing light put an end to the fighting at Ligny, and darkness covered the disorganized flight of numerous bodies to the northward and along the road to Namur. The 12th Brigade showed a bold front at Sombreffe, and behind it gradually assembled the bulk of Thielmann's corps. Further to the west a strong rear-guard was rallied at Bry, and covered the retirement of the right wing. The Field-Marshal was nowhere to be found, and all eyes were turned on Gneisenau, on whom by virtue of his seniority the command devolved. A decision as to the line of retreat had at once to be made. It was possible for the 3rd Corps, supported by the intact command of Bülow, to fall back either on Namur or Liège. But to deal with the right wing was a matter of great difficulty. The 1st and 2nd Corps had borne the brunt of the battle; their losses were heavy, and order was only partially restored. It would be impossible to retire across the front of the French line along the Namur road. There only remained the Roman road leading by Gembloux on Maestricht and Liège, and a route more directly northwards towards Wavre.

Order for Retreat R. 226 At a meeting of the Generals to the north of Bry, Gneisenau gave the order to retire on Tilly, but when his attention was called to the fact that Tilly was not marked on the maps, further indicated Wavre as the general line of retirement. Measures were at once taken to head off from Gembloux the fugitives on the Roman road, and restore order on the country roads leading from the chaussée northwards. The Head Quarters for the night were moved to Mellery, where Blücher was found much shaken by his fall, but otherwise not materially injured. The bulk of the 1st and 2nd Corps bivouacked in the country round Tilly and Mellery, but masses of fugitives pressed further northwards in great disorder.

L. V. 373

Staff officers were despatched along the narrow and crowded roads to rally the troops, but it was not till daylight that the flying columns were checked in the Huzelle forest some three miles south of Wavre. The Prussian army had meanwhile regained their leader, and orders signed by Grolmann were issued from Mellery directing a concentration of the whole army round Wavre. The 1st Corps were to move on Bierges, the 2nd Corps on St. Anne and Aisemont, the 3rd Corps through Wavre on La Bavette, and the 4th Corps on Dion-le-Mont. Immediate steps were taken to open up a new line of communication through Louvain to Maestricht and the Rhine fortresses, and ensure the renewal of warlike stores.

Movement on Wavre

THE PRUSSIAN RETREAT

H. 240 The decision to retire northwards towards Wavre had momentous consequences, "It was the decisive movement of the century." The choice of the line of retreat has been extolled as a strategical conception worthy of eternal remembrance, and one that fully compensated for the blundering arrangements of the day. The action taken by Gneisenau was endorsed a few hours later by Blücher, and

L. V. 344 few will agree in the opinion—unsupported by any trustworthy evidence—that the cautious head of the Staff had simply the intention of assembling his widely dispersed corps at Tilly within an hour's march of the victorious French army.

Comments The danger of the movement has been much exaggerated. Wavre was a position that could be easily defended, and although one line of communication was abandoned, another was opened through Louvain to the fortresses lower down the Rhine. In a populous and fertile country like Belgium supplies of food for a few days presented no great difficulty, while ammunition trains could be forwarded to the army with but little delay.

A retreat on Wavre rendered a union with the Anglo-Dutch army possible, but, as afterwards became evident, Gneisenau had no intention of endangering his own prospects for the benefit of an ally whom he undoubtedly distrusted. It was not a case of "breaking down the bridges behind him" in loyalty to a promise, but rather a destruction of bridges as a desirable temporary resort with the certainty of being able to build new ones the next day.

The retirement in a northerly direction was a wise

compromise. The danger was not great, the advantages might be enormous, and it was above all in accordance with the general plan that had been agreed upon with Wellington. The interpretation of Gneisenau's views by Thielmann was probably correct, i.e. that a retreat on Wavre was made with the ultimate intention of falling back on Maestricht. It would be ungenerous to criticize too closely the despatch that related the disaster at Ligny, but it makes clear how completely Gneisenau failed to grasp the strategical situation. It appeared to him that Napoleon was more likely to march on Liège and the Rhine than make a serious attempt to deal with Wellington.

L. V. 526

In the early morning of June 17, the 1st and 2nd Corps, leaving their scattered bivouacs, took the road by Gentinnes and Mont St. Guibert on Wavre. Two regiments of cavalry remained at Tilly to cover the retreat, and a mixed force of the three arms was for the same purpose temporarily left at Mont St. Guibert. On arriving near Wavre, Zieten crossed the Dyle and rested at Bierges, while Pirch I formed his corps in position close to Aisemont. Thielman with the 3rd Corps reached Gembloux at 6 a.m., and, taking up a position north of the village, formed a rallying point for some of the dispersed troops of the right wing. It was not till 2 p.m. that the march northwards was resumed by way of Corbais, and the troops were passing through Wavre as night fell. The rearguard did not arrive till after midnight, and bivouacked on the right bank of the Dyle.

Movement in detail

Bülow, with the 4th Corps, starting from Baudeset, marched by way of Walhain and Tourinnes to Dion-le-

Mont, where he arrived late at night. The artillery trains of reserve ammunition, about which some anxiety had been felt, reached Wavre at about five o'clock in the afternoon.

Nothing can be finer than the spirit displayed by the Prussians in their retirement, and on the day succeeding a disastrous defeat, a force of 90,000 men, in fairly good order with ample ammunition and some supplies, were assembled around Wavre.

The rear-guard had not been attacked during the march, and the enemy had apparently lost touch with the main Prussian army.

Messages between Allies At noon it was known that Wellington was retiring from Quatre-Bras, and that it was his intention to fight in front of the Soignes forest if Blücher would support him with one or two corps. Messages passed between the Head Quarters of the Allied armies during the day, and it is probable that even late at night assurances were given of the desire of the Field-Marshal to co-operate with the Duke to the best of his ability. Blücher after his disastrous defeat had still the utmost confidence in his troops. " I shall immediately lead you against the enemy " is to be found in the army order of the morning of June 17. There is a circumstantial account of the reception by the Duke in the evening of the 17th of a message that not only one corps but the whole Prussian army would come to his assistance.[1]

L. V. 360

Sib. 306

---

[1] Sib. I. 279 (first edition); Damitz. I, 222. It is suggested that Blücher, in his ignorance of the situation of his army, would not be justified in sending such a message, and that it is confused with the

It was not till 11 p.m. that a definite statement arrived from Müffling that Wellington had taken up a position at Mont St. Jean. The arrival of Bülow's corps had not been reported, and at the Prussian Head Quarters a heated discussion took place as to the best course to be adopted. Gneisenau had a genuine distrust of Wellington, and believed that he had designedly left the Prussians in the lurch at Ligny. He urged the advantage of falling back on Liège, and pointed out the danger that would follow a flank march towards the English in the event of the Duke being defeated. Grolmann supported the views of the Field-Marshal, and in the end Blücher had his way. "Gneisenau has given in," he said; "we are to march to join Wellington."

R. 230

A despatch was sent at midnight to Müffling, stating that at daybreak Bülow's corps would advance from Dion-le-Mont through Wavre on St. Lambert to attack the enemy in flank, and that the second corps would immediately follow it. The 1st and 3rd Corps would hold themselves in readiness to support the movement. "I beg for early information as to when and how the Duke is attacked, so that I may take measures accordingly."

L. V. 365
Decision to join Wellington

At 9.30 a.m. on the 18th a second despatch was forwarded to the effect that

H. 290

letter undoubtedly sent at 9.30 a.m. on the 18th instant. It seems quite possible, however, that some sort of assurance might have been sent in the afternoon if we consider that Blücher only estimated Grouchy's force as some 15,000 men (cf. L. V. 367; R. 230, 238). It is difficult otherwise to explain the conduct of Wellington in taking no measures to provide for a possible retreat from a dangerous position.

Blücher would lead his army in person, and was of opinion that in case the enemy did not attempt to advance both armies should fall upon him the following day. A postscript was added by Gneisenau entreating Müffling to make sure that the Duke was making a definite stand, as a mere demonstration on his part would seriously compromise the Prussian army. Orders were issued in the night for the 4th Corps of Bülow at Dion-le-Mont to start at daybreak for St. Lambert by way of Wavre, and for the 2nd Corps of Pirch I to follow the movement. The troops of Zieten and Thielmann which had crossed the Dyle were to remain in their bivouacs pending reports as to the advance of Grouchy. The corps of Bülow was chosen to lead the march as it had not been engaged at Ligny, but it was the furthest from the battlefield. There appears to have been considerable delay in moving off, and the vanguard did not reach Wavre till seven o'clock. Much time was lost defiling through the steep and narrow street, and a fire that broke out further delayed the main body for two hours. At noon the leading troops were massing at St. Lambert, but the tail of the column did not arrive till three o'clock. Much time might have been saved by skirting the town instead of passing through it.

Orders for the March

H. 289
The March on Waterloo

The 2nd Corps of Pirch I at Aisemont was under arms at 5 a.m., but its front was not cleared by Bülow till eleven o'clock, and only half the corps was across the Dyle at two o'clock. About noon an order was sent to the 1st Corps to march on Ohain, but the troops at Bierges were bivouacked mainly to the south of the main Wavre-St. Lambert road. Hence the line of march of the 4th and 2nd Corps had to be crossed. The various accounts are conflicting, but it seems probable that the advanced guard of Zieten was able to insert itself between the marching columns, and that the remainder of his troops were delayed till the 2nd Corps had passed.[1] Resulting from these very defective Staff arrangements and the abnormal delays on the march, the two leading divisions of the 4th Corps did not emerge from the wood of Paris till 4.30 p.m., while the weak division of Steinmetz only reached Ohain at 6 p.m.

Defective Staff Orders
Muf. Hist. 67

Wellington undoubtedly expected the arrival of Blücher in the early forenoon. " It had been planned that the Prussian army should attack about two o'clock." The arrangements of the Prussian Staff were such as to lead to the maximum of delay, and, after their own experiences at Ligny, they dallied with fortune in assuming that the Duke, with a weak composite force, could hold out till evening. " At any rate it was very questionable conduct to lead the Duke to expect help by midday, and to withhold the arrival of any direct succour until the evening *without warning him of that postponement.*"[2]

[1] Cf. L. V. 399, H. 399 and Pflugk. Harttung. "Das I Korps bei Belle-Alliance" (226). Had the 3rd Corps carried out its order to advance in support it would also have crossed the main line of march.

[2] *Napoleonic Studies*, Rose 288.

THE PURSUIT BY GROUCHY

CHAPTER XIV

THE PURSUIT BY GROUCHY

Reports from Outposts—Advance of Cavalry—March on Gembloux—Situation on Night of 17th—Advance on Corbais—Despatch to Emperor—Gérard and Grouchy—Comments—Advance on Wavre—Letter from Soult.

Reports from Outposts THE sentries of the opposing armies on the night of June 16 stood in close proximity as darkness fell. An extraordinary want of vigilance was shown by the corps of Lobau, which had supplied the outposts, and had not taken part in the battle. The retreat of the Prussian rear-guard from Bry was not noticed, nor in the early morning of the 17th was there any attempt to send out patrols, or to reconnoitre the line of retreat of the Prussian right wing. On the other flank the cavalry were more on the alert, and Pajol, with two regiments of hussars, at early dawn galloped down the Namur road and captured a battery and some wagons, and dispersed their escort. No more fugitives were to be seen, and the cavalry halted at Les Isnes, whence patrols were sent in all directions. At midday the reports made it clear that the enemy were moving in a northerly direction, and the road by St. Denis on Louvain was followed. By this time Pajol was reinforced by the arrival of a third regiment of hussars, the infantry division of Teste, and two batteries.

H. 244

Advance of Cavalry

When Sombreffe was evacuated by Thielmann, a brigade of Exelmans' dragoons followed after Pajol, but, guided by the reports of the peasantry, turned towards Gembloux, where they were checked by the Prussian vedettes at about 9 a.m. Soon after Exelmans arrived with the remainder of his cavalry, and justly estimated that a whole Prussian corps was bivouacked to the north of the village. No attempt was made to push back the Prussian cavalry, nor was the very important information that had been acquired reported either to Grouchy,[1] Pajol, or the Emperor till the afternoon. Exelmans at 10 a.m. was in the presence of a large body of the enemy, while Pajol had acquired the negative information that nothing was taking place on the roads leading to Namur. Had the facts been known at Head Quarters, it would have cleared up the situation sufficiently to enable the Emperor to give more definite orders for the pursuit.

March on Gembloux

Grouchy, after leaving the Emperor at about half-past eleven, sent orders to Vandamme (at St. Amand) to at once march on Point-du-Jour, while he proceeded to Ligny to personally order Gérard to follow the route of the 3rd Corps towards Gembloux. The delay that ensued is almost incredible. The 4th Corps could not move till the 3rd Corps had defiled past it, and the latter marched at a most leisurely pace. The leading infantry did not reach Point-du-Jour till three o'clock, and after a long halt

---

[1] Information as to the presence of the Prussian corps was not received by Grouchy till 3 p.m. (H. 250).

the column proceeded to Gembloux, and began to form up at six o'clock in the evening. Though the infantry had accomplished but a short march, and two hours of daylight remained, Grouchy ordered Vandamme to encamp around the village, with Gérard to the south of it. The Prussians had long since disappeared, and the only excuse given for not continuing the movement was the rainy weather and the bad condition of the roads.

The main task of Grouchy was to clear up the situation and to determine the line of the enemy's retreat. Nothing was known as to the Prussian right wing, and yet during the hours occupied by the slow progress of the infantry, not a cavalry patrol was sent forward towards Gentinnes or Mont St. Guibert. Grouchy, the commander of a cavalry corps, marched with his infantry, and the only information he received before reaching Gembloux was, at 3 p.m., a belated letter from Exelmans, stating that he was observing the enemy and would follow them up when they moved;

H. 253

and, at 6 p.m., a note from Pajol, that the enemy appeared to be marching on Louvain.

Meanwhile, during the slow advance of the French infantry, Thielmann, at about 2 p.m., retired northward under cover of a rear-guard, and it was not till three o'clock that Exelmans' dragoons entered Gembloux. Instead of at once following up the traces of the enemy, the French cavalry, content with capturing a herd of oxen, marched to Sauvenières, from whence, at 6 p.m., a brigade was sent northwards beyond Sart-à-Walhain, and a regiment of dragoons towards Perwez. It was late at night when Grouchy received the reports of the reconnoitring cavalry from Nil St. Vincent, Tourinnes and Perwez, the main purport of which was that the Prussian troops were retiring on Wavre. The cavalry bivouacked at night at Ernage and Sauvenières.

H. 253

Situation on Night of 17th   The situation, as it appeared to Grouchy on the evening of the 17th, based on Pajol's despatch and the information of the inhabitants, is described in his despatch to the Emperor, dated 10 p.m., at Gembloux. "It seems, from all the reports, that the enemy on arriving at Sauvenières, divided into two columns, one taking the Wavre road through Sart-à-Walhain, the other heading on Perwez. One may infer that a portion is going to join Wellington, that the centre, under Blücher, is retiring on Liège, while another column had effected its retreat on Namur." The orders for the next day (June 18), for the 3rd and 4th Corps to proceed to Sart-à-Wilhain, make it clear that it was in the direction of Liège that Grouchy intended to seek the enemy.

App. 12

But during the night the reports from the cavalry, strengthened by further information at 3 a.m. from the neighbourhood of Walhain, made it clear that the Prussian army was moving on Wavre.

H. 257

Writing to Pajol at daybreak, he states, "the movement of retreat of Blücher's army appears to me very clearly to be upon Brussels."

R. 251

The situation was now clear. The Prussian army had retired on Wavre with the probable intention of taking the road to Brussels. It was, however, possible that they would move westward to join the English army in front of the forest of Soignes. To meet both contingencies, it was advisable to press the enemy as closely as possible, and secure the bridges over the Dyle. There was everything to gain and nothing to lose by moving towards the banks of the river. Wavre could be more easily attacked, the pursuit to Brussels could be more readily carried out, and, above all, the junction between the Allied Prussian and English armies would be hindered.[1]

Grouchy was, however, unequal to the situation, and although he decided to march on Wavre, he made no alteration in his orders of the evening of June 17.

Advance on Corbais A servile persistence in following up the rear-guard of the enemy by a long detour was a strategical blunder, which could only be remedied by rapidity and vigour in pursuit. At three o'clock in the morning it was quite light enough to march, and yet Grouchy gave the order for Vandamme to start at 6 a.m., and for Gérard to follow him at 8 a.m. Owing to delays in the distribution of rations, the march did not commence till nearly eight o'clock, and the error of the previous day, of making both corps follow the same route, was repeated. Grouchy apparently marched with the infantry, and on reaching Walhain about ten o'clock, stopped to breakfast and wrote a report to the Emperor. The corps of

H. 295

---

[1] Jomini, Clausewitz and Charras unite in the opinion that Grouchy should have marched in the early morning to Moustier, which might have been reached at 10 a.m. What the ultimate result would have been is a matter of conjecture. It seems probable that Grouchy would be engaged with a portion of the Prussian army, while the remainder would reinforce the left flank of Wellington. Owing to the superiority in numbers of the Allied armies, it would be difficult to obtain a victory; but a defeat so disastrous to the French army as that of Waterloo might be averted (cf. Ropes, Grouard, Houssaye).

Vandamme, followed by that of Gérard, meanwhile was moving through the village on Corbais and Wavre, while Exelmans' cavalry, well in advance, was scouting in the Huzelle wood.

Despatch to Emperor

App. 13

The despatch of Grouchy to the Emperor, dated 11 a.m., states that the 1st, 2nd and 3rd Corps of Blücher's army are marching in the direction of Brussels. "This evening I expect to be concentrated at Wavre, and thus place myself between Wellington, whom I presume to be in retreat before Your Majesty, and the Prussian army." It is not easy to understand exactly what Grouchy meant. He appears to have in his mind the statement made to him by an old officer residing at Walhain, that some of the Prussians were moving on La Chyse, and also probably thought that any junction with the English would be preceded by a retirement towards Brussels.

The despatch of 11 a.m. had hardly been delivered to the bearer when the sound of a distant cannonade was heard. Gérard, in advance of his corps, now appeared on the scene with his Staff.

Gérard and Grouchy

H. 301

The dull reports in rapid succession were followed by clouds of smoke on the horizon. There was no longer a doubt that a great battle was in progress.

"We must march to the cannon," said Gérard, and his words were echoed by General Valazé.

"The battle is at Mont St. Jean," said the peasant guide. "We could get there in four or five hours." The notary, who was present, confirmed the guide. "It is on the edge of the forest of Soignes."

Grouchy admits that he was vexed that his subordinates should give this unasked-for advice so frankly. He explained that the Emperor intended to attack the English Army, and that if he wished for assistance he would have said so. Besides, owing to the distance, it would be impossible to arrive in time to do any good.

Gérard grew the more insistent:

"Monsieur le Maréchal, it is your duty to march to the cannon." Offended at the rebuke, Grouchy replied:

"My duty is to execute the Emperor's orders, which direct me to follow the Prussians."

At this moment, about noon, arrived an aide-de-camp from Exelmans, who reported that a strong rear-guard of the enemy was posted in front of Wavre, and that there was every indication that the Prussians were in movement towards the English army. So evident did this appear that General Exelmans proposed to cross to the left bank of the Dyle at Ottignies.

Telling the bearer of the despatch that he would himself give orders to the cavalry, Grouchy called for his charger. As he put his foot in the stirrup Gérard made a last appeal:

"If you will not go to Soignes, let me take my corps there, and I may arrive in time to be useful."

"No," replied Grouchy, "I cannot break up my command." And he forthwith set out at a gallop towards Wavre.

Comments
L. V. 393
The decision to keep all his troops united was no doubt correct, but it is a matter of dispute as to what would have happened if the first advice of Gérard to march to the sound of the firing had been adopted. Assuming that no resistance

was offered, the valley of the Lasne might be reached by seven o'clock; but it would then be too late to materially affect the fighting at Waterloo. It was probable, however, that the movement of the pursuing force would be checked by in front two or three divisions of the II Prussian Corps, while on the flank was Thielmann, and possibly some of the troops of Zieten. The French would necessarily be marching in a long column over bad roads, and any attack, even by cavalry, would cause serious delay. To co-operate with the Emperor on the 18th, it was necessary to start from Gembloux in the early morning. At noon it was too late to do more than be of assistance in covering his retreat.

<small>L. V. 404
H. 507
R. 260</small>

Between nine and ten o'clock the scouts of Exelmans' cavalry had come in contact with a Prussian force of the three arms on the heights south of Wavre. The dragoons accordingly fell back towards Corbais, leaving an advanced guard at La Baraque, while one brigade was sent to Neuf Sart on the right, and another to Ottignies on the left, for the purposes of reconnaissance. When Grouchy overtook Vandamme's corps, at Nil St. Vincent at one o'clock, orders were at once given to the cavalry and the leading infantry divisions to advance by the main road through the Huzelle wood. While this movement was in progress and a little before two o'clock, the advanced guard at La Baraque was attacked and driven off the road by a regiment of Prussian hussars advancing from the south-west. As the main body of the dragoons appeared on the scene, the enemy's cavalry fell back on Wavre, and were covered

<small>Advance on Wavre</small>

<small>H 458</small>

from pursuit by infantry skirmishers lining the road. The enemy, who had so unexpectedly appeared on the scene, were the cavalry and infantry of Ledebur's detachment, which had been left in observation at Mont St. Guibert. The Prussian commander, on realizing that his retreat was cut off, had made a bold dash northwards over country tracks and regained contact with his main body. It is a matter for surprise that the French cavalry should not be aware of the presence of Prussian troops within a mile and a half of its main line of advance, but that a detachment expressly posted to give warning of the approach of a pursuing enemy should so completely neglect its functions is almost unexampled in warfare.

The advance of Vandamme's infantry soon led to a fierce wood fight with Ledebur's battalions, which were reinforced from the main body. Grouchy directed the whole of the dragoons towards Dion-le-Mont to effect a turning movement, but before it could take effect the Prussians had evacuated the wood and fell back on Wavre.

The dull boom of a distant cannonade was still heard, and Grouchy, in impatience, galloped westward to Limelette when he at last became assured that a great battle was in progress. On returning to the Wavre road he received, between 3.30 and 4 p.m., the letter despatched by Soult from Le Caillou at ten o'clock, enjoining him to march on Wavre and draw closer to the main army.[1] A report

<small>H. 461
Letter from Soult</small>

---

[1] "Ainsi Sa Majesté désire que vous dirigiez vos movements sur Wavre, afin de vous rapprocher de nous, vous mettre en rapport d'operations et lier les communications," etc. (App. 14).

at the same time came in from the cavalry on the right flank that no trace of the enemy was found to the eastward.

Orders were at once sent to Pajol to despatch his hussars and the Teste division to Limale, where he was to force the passage of the Dyle.

To link together the communications of the two French armies it was necessary to capture the bridges above Wavre. No time had to be lost, and yet Grouchy sent orders to a force ten miles distant while the cavalry and leading division of Gérard's corps was already within an hour's march of the Dyle.

H. 463

THE BATTLE OF WATERLOO

CHAPTER XV

THE BATTLE OF WATERLOO

Description of Position—Scheme of Occupation—The Troops Available—The Front Line—The Advanced Posts—The Reserves—The Force at Hal—Napoleon's Order for the Advance—Letter to Grouchy—The French Deployment—Attack on Hougoumont—Preparation for Main Attack—Second Letter to Grouchy—Attack on Centre of Position—Charge of Household Brigade—Charge of Union Brigade—Fighting at La Haie and Hougoumont—First Cavalry Attack—Second Charge—Third Charge—Fourth Charge—Advance of Foy—Prussian Advance on Planchenoit—Attack of La Haie Sainte—Recapture of Planchenoit—Approach of Zieten—Attack by the Guard—Retreat of the Guard—The Prussian Flank Attack—The Rout—The Pursuit.

Description of Position THE main road to Charleroi ran due south from Brussels through the beech forest of Soignes. At the hamlet of Mont St. Jean —some two miles beyond the village of Waterloo—the chaussée to Nivelles branched off to the south-west. The terrain here rose in gentle incline to the cross-road from Ohain to Braine l'Alleud, which marked the front of the English position. Separated from the plateau of Mont St. Jean by two shallow valleys, and at some 1,400 yards from it, lay the rising ground on which the Imperial army formed for attack. To the westward of the main road a level spur connected the two positions, while the valley at Hougoumont branched abruptly northwards towards Merbe-Braine.

The Ohain road afforded considerable facilities for defence. To the eastward of the chaussée it ran level with the soil, but for some 700 yards a border of high and thick hedges formed an obstacle of some importance. To the westward the ground rises, and the lane for some 400 yards became a cutting, which afforded cover to men standing upright.

In advance of the right lay the chateau of Hougoumont, with its walled garden and enclosed orchard and copses, while the stone buildings of La Haie Sainte, its terraced kitchen garden and the sand-pit, formed a strong guard-post to the main road. To the eastward the hamlets of Papelotte, La Haye and Smohain afford cover and lodgment for troops advanced in front of the left flank.

The position was well suited for defensive purposes. On the ridge behind the advanced posts there was good cover for the front line, while the reverse slope concealed from view the second line and reserves. Every movement of the enemy could plainly be seen, and every approach was dominated by fire.[1] "Except a line of skirmishers halfway down the slope, with a few batteries of artillery in support, there was nothing to be seen . . . no shelter trenches standing out against the skyline defined the front. It was impossible to detect the extent of the English line, for outlying detachments, pushed far out on either hand, stood in the path of patrols." The whole area of the battlefield was covered by crops of ripening rye, and the heavy soil, saturated with rain, made all rapid movement, even of cavalry, a matter of great difficulty. The advisability of choosing a battlefield in front of a forest admits of

[1] *Notes on Wellington.* (Henderson.)

argument. Wellington maintained that as it was open enough for the passage of the three arms it was very defensible. But he definitely states [1]: " I never contemplated a retreat on Brussels," but would have retired either towards Wavre on the Prussians or by his right to the coast.

Scheme of Occupation
The rain did not cease till 4 a.m., and the night was passed in great discomfort. In the morning the troops, after unloading their muskets, cleaning their accoutrements and preparing their food, were led by Staff officers to their appointed places in the line of battle. The general scheme was to hold with infantry and artillery the line of the Ohain road from its junction with the Nivelles road as far as the lane leading to Verd Cocu. The extreme left, where the ground was open and level, was to be occupied by cavalry, and the approach to it protected by strong advanced posts in the villages on the Ohain stream. Wellington was apprehensive of being turned by his right, and secured it by placing most of his infantry reserves on that flank. Especial attention was also directed to Hougoumont and its enclosures, which were placed in a state of defence on the night of June 17-18. The garrisons of La Haie Sainte and of the hamlets in front of the left flank were left to take their own measures for protection, and in the main line of defence little was done except to cut passages through the hedges and sunken road for the use of the guns.

[1] Chesney, 197; Max, i. 48. The direction of retirement would depend on the result of the battle, but the contingency of being wholly or partially forced to retire on the coast gives some colour to the supposition that the detachment at Hal was meant to lend assistance to such a movement.

[1] Working parties had been detailed to throw up epaulments for the guns, but practically nothing was done in the way of entrenchment. The abattis raised on the Charleroi and Nivelles road were of little practical value.

The troops available The army of the Duke on the field at Waterloo was composed as follows:—

Infantry	49,608
Cavalry	12,408
Artillery	5,645
Total	[2] 67,661 men with 158 guns.

The troops were of many nationalities, viz:—

British	23,991
King's German Legion	5,824
Hanoverians	11,247
Brunswickers	5,935
Nassauers	2,880
Dutch-Belgians	17,784
Total	67,661 men.

The veterans of the Peninsula were troops of the highest class, but, including cavalry, did not amount to 20,000 men. Many of the British troops were recruits, the Hanoverians and Brunswickers were raw, recently raised and imperfectly disciplined bodies, while the Dutch-Belgian and [3] Nassau contingents were not above suspicion for various causes. Wellington did not conceal his dissatisfaction with his command; it was [4] "the worst equipped army with the worst staff

---

[1] Chesney, 220. Engineers were ordered from Hal to throw up entrenchments at Braine-l'Alleud, but the work was not carried out.

[2] Sibborne, i. 460; De Bas, iii. 684.

[3] The Nassau battalions came over from Soult's army at Bayonne in 1813. The seasoned portions of the Belgian army had served under Napoleon.

[4] "I had only about 35,000 men on whom I could rely. . . If

ever brought together." In allotting the troops to their various positions it was necessary to mix the various nationalities so as to neutralize the weakness of a composite force. No attempt was made to adhere to the army corps organization, and even the divisional commands were not in all cases kept intact.

The Front Line
[1] The nine infantry brigades occupying the front were 22,000 strong, and were composed of a first line of twenty-four battalions and a second line of fourteen battalions. The normal formation for battle was two deployed lines, and the battalions when not in line were formed in columns of companies at quarter distance. The disposition of the 3rd Division, which occupied the ground to the immediate west of the Charleroi road, may be studied with interest. Instead of the ordinary square formation to resist cavalry, it was arranged that oblongs with a front of four companies and a side of one company should be used. In the case of battalions weak in numbers, two joined together to form an oblong. The onslaught of the French cavalry was thus received by five oblongs in front line with the four, in second line so disposed as to stand opposite the [2] intervals of the columns to their front.

The extreme left of the line, where the ground was quite open, was held by Vivian and Vandeleur's brigades of cavalry, some 2,300 strong. The abrupt termination of the ridge by a short steep slope into the valley lead-

I had the same army as in the south of France, the battle would have been won in three hours " (Wellington to Jones, 1819; Porter's *History of R.E.* i. 382). Shaw-Kennedy (57) estimates the Allied army as a force equivalent to 41,000 British troops.

[1] One battalion of Krause's Nassau regiment is counted in second line, while the battalions of Saxe-Weimar are excluded.

[2] Shaw-Kennedy, 101.

ing towards Merbe-Braine marked the extreme right of the main position. Here Mitchell's brigade (4th Division) — some 1,700 strong — was posted, with two battalions acting as a support to a number of companies thrown forward to hold the lane leading from Hougoumont to Braine l'Alleud. The anxiety of the Duke as to an attack on his right flank was further evidenced by his detachment of the whole of Chassé's Dutch-Belgian division to Braine l'Alleud, which lay about a mile distant in the right rear of his main line of defence.

In support of the infantry along the line of the Ohain road were at first posted ten batteries of artillery. One troop commanded the Charleroi chaussée, while the remaining troops and foot-batteries were distributed on suitable sites to the eastward and westward of it. The total force was some fifty-two guns [1] in front line, but as only eighteen guns were at Mont St. Jean and sixteen with Chassé's division, the bulk of the artillery was in close support in rear. At one o'clock ninety-six guns were in action, and before the close of the battle every battery had done some service. The chateau and enclosures of Hougoumont were held by 1,200 men composed of the light companies of the Guards division, a Nassau battalion of Saxe-Weimar's brigade, and a company of Hanoverians. Major Baring, with 400 men of the German Legion, occupied La Haie Sainte, while the Saxe-Weimar brigade (less one battalion) were posted in front of the left at Papelotte and Smohain. A line of sentries and piquets

The Advanced Posts

---

[1] Including the three guns of Stevenart in support of Saxe-Weimar and the seven guns of Byleveld's troop in rear of Bylandt's brigade (De Bas, iii. 684; *Waterloo*, Boulger, 20-22).

were pushed down the slopes and connected the advanced posts.

The main position at the commencement of the battle was occupied by a force of 31,000 men, of whom some 6,000 were detached to occupy the advanced posts in front of the right, centre and left of the line. A reference to the map will show the disposition of the supports and reserves. The space available was very limited, and the movements of the troops early in the battle explain the variations that occur in different plans and accounts. The division of Dutch-Belgian cavalry was placed in reserve near Mont St. Jean, together with three batteries of artillery and ammunition columns. The rest of the cavalry brigades, with their troops of artillery, formed a general second line of support. The 2nd Division of Clinton formed in rear of the right towards Merbe-Braine, while the Brunswick and Nassau troops lay behind the right centre. Lambert's brigade at an early stage moved from Mont St. Jean to a position in rear of the left centre of the line. The Dutch-Belgian division of Chassé, which was at first detached to Braine l'Alleud, was moved in the course of the battle to join the reserves in rear of the right. The distribution of the Duke's army at 11 a.m. may be summarized as follows:—

The Reserves

In advanced posts	6,000 men.
In front line (with supports)	25,000 ,,
In second line (cavalry)	6,800 ,,
Reserve in rear of right	15,000 ,,
Reserve in rear of centre	7,800 ,,
Detached division on right	7,100 ,,
Total	67,700 men.

The Force at Hal.
H. 176

The retention by Wellington during the battle of a force of 18,000 men at Hal has been condemned by all critics. It may be urged that the Duke on June 17 and 18 could not know that Napoleon had detached his right wing in pursuit of the Prussians. The whole French army might be advancing against him, and in such a case the detachment of a force by way of Hal to operate against his communications was not impossible. But on the morning of the 18th the situation was changed. There were no reports as to the presence of French troops on the Mons and Nivelles roads, Napoleon had massed apparently all his troops at Belle Alliance, and, instead of the single Prussian corps asked for, Blucher had promised to bring his whole army. Any wide turning movement could only be undertaken by cavalry in weak numbers, and it was not necessary to keep a mixed force of 18,000 men with thirty guns to meet a very improbable contingency. At any rate, Colville's troops at Tubize could easily be spared by Prince Frederick. The idea of Müffling that troops superfluous at Waterloo might be very effective if Napoleon's retreat by Genappes and Nivelles was cut off is somewhat far-fetched, but there is no doubt that Wellington trusted a great deal to the early support of the Prussian army. The Duke also had always the intention of retiring on the coast if defeated, and a force at Hal would be of assistance in covering such a movement.

[1] " Il se peut que l'ennemi nous tourne par Hal quoique le temps est terrible et les chemins detestables " (Letter of Wellington to Duc de Berri, June 18, 3 a.m.; Müffling's *Life*, 244; Kennedy, 69 Chesney, 218).

THE BATTLE OF WATERLOO 165

Napoleon's Order for the Advance The order of the Emperor that the line of battle was to be formed by nine o'clock could not be carried out. At daybreak on the 18th the bivouacs spread back as far as Genappes, and there was much delay in collecting the troops for a forward movement. The fields were so saturated by rain that it was difficult to march across country, and the main road was crowded by the advancing troops. While the sun and wind were drying the soil the Emperor rode to the outposts to examine the English position, and detailed an engineer officer to ascertain if it was entrenched. On returning to Rossomme he proceeded to answer[1] the letter of Grouchy, which stated that if the main Prussian army retired on Wavre, he would follow them " in order that they may not be able to reach Brussels, and to separate them from Wellington."

Letter to Grouchy Warning Grouchy that he is about to attack the English army at Waterloo, he enjoins him to " direct your movements on Wavre in order to draw closer to us, keep in touch with [2] the operations, and preserve contact with us." It is evident that at the hour of despatching the letter the Emperor neither summoned Grouchy to the battlefield, nor expected him to appear there, but trusted to his keeping the Prussians occupied. He also dismissed as " impossible " a report brought to him by his brother Jerome to the effect that a junction between the English and Prussian armies before the forest of

H. 323

---

[1] Despatched from Gembloux at 10 p.m. on June 17. The original has been tampered with, but there is no material difference between the two versions (R. 358; H. 256). App. 12.

[2] Soult to Grouchy, 10 a.m., June 18 (H. 325; App. 14).

Soignes was contemplated. But as a precautionary measure Marbot, with his hussars, was sent in reconnaisance eastward beyond the Lasne.

The French Deployment

The force now assembling for battle numbered some [1] 74,000 men with 246 guns. From the plateau of Mont St. Jean at 10 a.m. the undulating plain to the south seemed covered with advancing columns. In the sunlight " it was a kaleidoscope of vivid hues and metallic flashes." By eleven o'clock the front line, composed of the corps of D'Erlon and Reille, and flanked by cavalry, deployed on a curve extending from the Nivelles road to the south of Papelotte. In rear was forming the corps of Lobau flanked by the bulk of the cavalry, while as a reserve gradually came up the Imperial Guard and two divisions of cavalry. To each cavalry and infantry division was attached a battery of artillery, while [2] each army corps had an additional battery of heavy guns. The artillery reserve remained with the Imperial Guard. From flank to flank was nearly two and a half miles, and the front was not more than 1,400 yards from the main British line.

Vide Map

Napoleon was unwilling to attack until all his troops were formed up, but issued (at 11 a.m.) his instructions for massing a great battery opposite the centre of the English position to prepare the way for the advance of the corps of D'Erlon. It was difficult to estimate the strength of the Anglo-Dutch

H. 332

---

[1] Houssaye. Sibborne gives a total of 71,947 men. Oman points out that Houssaye underestimates the losses at Ligny.

[2] The ordinary equipment of a battery was six 6-pounder guns and two howitzers. Heavy batteries were composed of 12-pounders and howitzers.

army; but from the tenor of the order it was evident that the Emperor underrated the resistance that would be offered to him. A few minutes later a verbal order was sent to Reille to demonstrate towards Hougoumont, and thus induce Wellington to reinforce his right at the expense of the troops defending the centre of his line.

Attack on Hougoumont

At 11.50 a.m. the first cannon shot was fired by a battery of the 2nd Corps, and an artillery duel was commenced with the batteries on the English right.[1] One of Jerome's brigades, covered by skirmishers, descended into the valley, and gained a lodgment in the wood. Step by step the Nassau and Hanoverian troops were driven back. Reinforced by the light companies of the Guards, the defenders offered a gallant resistance, and it was nearly one o'clock before the attack was brought to a stand in front of the chateau and loopholed garden wall of Hougoumont. The English were well under shelter, and every shot told. Daring attempts were made to scale the wall and break in the door of the chateau, but without success. Jerome now called up his second brigade to relieve the assailants, who took ground to the left and assaulted the chateau on its western side. At the same time an entrance into the orchard was forced by the newly arrived supports. The attacks both on the eastern and western sides of the farm enclosure was repulsed by the advance of some companies of the Guards from the main line, and it was nearly two o'clock when the de-

---

[1] "The artillery was placed with orders not to engage with artillery, but to fire only when bodies of troops came under their fire. It was very difficult to get them to obey this order" (Max i. 74; Mercer i. 302).

cimated battalions withdrew to the cover of the wood. The views of the Emperor would have been carried out by the occupation of the wood, and the disregard by Jerome of the repeated orders of Reille to break off the action led to a waste of energy that had far-reaching results.

Preparation for the Main Attack

Meanwhile the supports and reserves of the French army had formed up in their allotted positions. It was one o'clock, and the troops stood eagerly waiting the order to advance. The Emperor was in a position of some difficulty. An unsatisfactory [1] despatch had been received from Grouchy showing that at 6 a.m. he was still at Gembloux. In the far horizon to the north-east a movement of troops was seen through the glasses of the Staff, and a Prussian subaltern of hussars had been captured near Lasne, who was the bearer of a letter to Wellington from Bülow announcing the arrival of his corps at Chapelle St. Lambert. In answer to Grouchy a letter was sent (1 p.m.) approving of the pursuit to Wavre, but enjoining manœuvring towards the main army, so as to intercept the westward march of any Prussian corps. [2] "At this moment a battle is taking place at Waterloo . . . so manœuvre to join our right." The interception of Bülow's letter caused a hasty postscript to be added: "Lose no time to draw near and join us and crush Bülow." The situation was more serious than Napoleon would to himself admit. Grouchy

---

[1] "Tous mes rapports et renseignments confirment que l'ennemi se retire sur Bruxelles. . . Ils doivent etre partis hier soir et avoir marché pendant toute la nuit" (Gembloux, 6 a.m.; H. 342).

[2] Appendix xv.

might either be containing the main Prussian army at Wavre, or, having given up the pursuit, might be moving on Planchenoit to the sound of the guns. In any case he would not receive Napoleon's letter in sufficient time to alter his arrangements.[1]

As a precautionary measure to protect the flank of the army, the light cavalry divisions of Domon and Subervie were detached to observe all approaches from the east, and Lobau received orders to move his corps to a suitable position for their support.

Attack on Centre of Position
At half-past one the great battery of eighty guns, massed opposite the centre of the English line, opened fire. After a cannonade of half an hour the four divisions of D'Erlon —with intervals of 400 yards between them—moved forward past the guns for the attack, the artillery fire playing over their heads. Their formation was somewhat unusual. The battalions, deployed in a three-deep line, were massed one behind another, and as the French battalions were weak, the divisions had in no case a front exceeding 200 men. Over the miry, rain-sodden soil the movement was slow, and the massive columns suffered severely from fire as they mounted the slope crowned by the English line.

Of Allix's division one brigade assaulted La Haie Sainte and drove the defenders out of the orchard. The remaining brigade obtained a success more to the eastward by the sand-pit. Wellington at once sent a battalion to aid in the defence of the farm buildings, and as it advanced to the westward of them it was charged by

[1] The route taken by the orderlies was via Quatre-Bras and the main road.

French cuirassiers, who, riding through the ranks, reached the edge of the plateau. Further to the eastward Bylandt's Dutch-Belgian brigade which, from its exposed position, had lost heavily from artillery fire, was unable to withstand the approach of Donzelot and Marcognet, and fell back in confusion.[1] On the right of the advance Durutte's column dislodged the defenders of Papelotte.

The columns of Allix, Donzelot and Marcognet were now close to the hedge lining the Ohain road. Lying down some 100 yards to the northward were the deployed brigades of Pack and Kempt. As soon as the French skirmishers became visible on the crest, the order was given to stand and advance. A bound forward, and from the southern hedge a volley was poured into the dense masses of Donzelot. The French recoiled, and Kempt's brigade charging in line forced a desperate bayonet fight. Further to the eastward Marcognet's column had gained the crest and road, and was decimated by the fire of Pack's advancing line.

Charge of Household Brigade It was now the turn of the cavalry. The Household brigade with the Blues in support charged in line between the squares of Alten's division against the French cuirassiers, who had reached the hollow road to the west of the main chaussée. With all the advantages of a descending slope, superior numbers and heavier horses, the English carried all before them, and in ungoverned pursuit charged up to the main French position. Nearly half the brigade eventu-

---

[1] According to De Bas the Bylandt brigade was in line with Pack and Kempt, and on retiring did good work in second line (Report of Van Zuylen; De Bas, 681, 684).

ally combined with the Union brigade in the charge on the great French battery, while the remainder, coming under the steady fire of Bachelu's division, fell back with much depleted numbers under the protection of the Blues, who alone were well kept in hand.

Charge of Union Brigade. From the rear of Picton's division the three regiments of the Union brigade at the same time galloped forward. Irregularity of formation arose from the difficulty of passing the infantry and the hedges, but the horsemen fell impetuously on the paralysed and unwieldly masses of the French divisions.

The columns were shattered and hurled down the slope, and some 3,000 men were taken to the rear as prisoners by Picton's division. In their headlong career across the valley the cavalry cut down two batteries that had been following the French advance, and then swept on till they rode into the great French battery. All regular formations were lost, there were no supports, and the exhausted horsemen fell an easy prey to the lances of Jaquinot and the cuirassiers of Milhaud.

More to the eastward and after some delay,[1] Vandeleur with two regiments charged down the slope towards Durutte's division, which effected its retreat in fairly good order. The troops were ordered not to go beyond the bottom of the valley, and supported by a Dutch-Belgian regiment, covered the retirement of the remnants of the Union brigade. The slopes of the valley, so recently the scene of combat, were now literally covered by the killed and wounded, and a brief period of calm ensued.[2] Wellington moved up Lambert's

[1] Müffling's *Life*, 245.   [2] Kennedy, 112.

brigade to the right of Picton's depleted ranks, and reinforced the garrison of La Haie Sainte by two companies. Napoleon had grave cause for anxiety. During the heat of the action a letter was received from Grouchy, dated 11 a.m., stating that he would be at Wavre in the evening, and showing that he apparently was not inquieting himself as to what was taking place on the Charleroi road. But Walhain was, as the crow flies, more than twenty miles from the battlefield, and Bülow was already massing his troops five miles off. At the best it might be hoped that Grouchy would march to the sound of the firing, and thus fall on the rear of Bülow, or at all events hold in check the other corps of the Prussian army. No time had to be lost.

Fighting at La Haie and Hougoumont

As soon as D'Erlon could rally his battalions (about 3.30 p.m.), they were ordered again to attack La Haie Sainte and the centre of the position with two brigades. The attempt was a failure, and the troops fell back to the bottom of the valley.

Throughout the afternoon there had been an unceasing contest at Hougoumont. The assailants and defenders had both been reinforced. The wood and orchard had again been taken and the farm buildings set on fire, but the English still tenaciously held the chateau and the walled garden. At about four o'clock there was a terrific burst of fire from the French batteries. "Never," said General Alten, "had the oldest soldiers heard such a cannonade." The withdrawal under cover of some of the English troops in front line was mistaken as a movement of retreat, and Ney, without orders from the Emperor, massed the cuirassiers of Milhaud and the light cavalry divisions of Lefebvre-Desnouettes, which were in rear of D'Erlon's corps, for a great cavalry attack. The movement was premature, and directed against the most strongly held portion of the Duke's position.

First Cavalry Attack, 4 p.m. Across the valley between Hougoumont and La Haie rode forty squadrons in lines of squadron columns. The rye crop on the sodden soil checked the pace, and as, at a slow canter, they breasted the slope, repeated volleys of case from the English batteries depleted the ranks. Line after line gained the crest, and, sweeping through the guns, fell in quick succession on the squares of the infantry.

Wellington had moved up a part of his reserves to the threatened point, and now volleys of musketry from sixteen squares strewed the ground with the brave horsemen. Against the disordered masses the Duke hurled the cavalry of the Anglo-German, Brunswick and Belgian brigades, and drove them off the plateau. Some of the horsemen only withdrew below the crest, and menaced the guns whenever an attempt was made to reload them.[1]

Second Charge Reforming in the valley some two-thirds of the squadrons were again led to the charge in a similar gallant but unsuccessful effort. The Emperor at Belle Alliance realized the terrible blunder that had been made. "There is a premature movement," he said to Soult,

---

[1] Throughout the battle no attempt was made by either French or English cavalry to spike or otherwise dismantle temporarily captured guns.

H. 375 "which may produce fatal results. It is too early by an hour, but we must back up what we have done."

Third Charge

H. 382

An order was at once sent for Kellermann and Guyot to advance. As the heavy cavalry debouched in the valley they were joined by the defeated horsemen that still remained effective, and some sixty [1] squadrons in successive lines surged over the crest. For an instant the squares seemed overwhelmed, but as the smoke cleared they reappeared as if rooted to the ground. The ranks, at times broken by falling horses, were at once reformed. "We had the French cavalry walking about us as if they had been our own. I never saw the British infantry behave so well." In rear of the second line the drivers and horses of the ammunition wagons were cut down, but beyond this there was very little further success. The murderous fire of the infantry and the repeated charges of Grant's squadrons at last forced the exhausted horsemen to fall back slowly and reluctantly into the valley. After reforming and calling up Blancard's brigade, Ney at the head of the carbineers led once more a charge for the fourth time. But the squadrons had lost half their strength, and the men were demoralized. The plateau was again gained, but the attack failed in vigour, and the worn-out cavalry, after their last attempt, fell back to the southern [2] slope of the valley. It was

Fourth Charge
H. 376

---

[1] A brigade of carbineers was temporarily retained in reserve by Kellermann, but took part in the next charge (H. 376).

[2] Interesting details as to the French cavalry attack may be gleaned from *Mercer's Journal* and from Sir E. Wood's *Cavalry in the Waterloo Campaign*.

now six o'clock. During this phase of the cavalry combat (4 to 6 p.m.) there was a desultory action taking place at both La Haie Sainte and Hougoumont. No attempt had been made to support the cavalry in its attack, and yet they had at hand more than a division of infantry of Reille's corps. The subsequent advance of the infantry under Bachelu and Foy was made too late. As they ascended the slope encumbered by dead and wounded, they were swept down by the converging fire of artillery and infantry. "It was a hail of death."

Advance of Foy

H. 388

Meanwhile the Prussians were slowly advancing from Wavre. Between ten and eleven o'clock their cavalry was discerned in the direction of Ohain, and it was hoped that they would take part in the battle between one and two o'clock.[1] The main body of Bülow's corps at Chapelle St. Lambert was joined by Blücher at one o'clock, and after waiting some time for the reports of scouts, he started the troops in the direction of Planchenoit. The Field-Marshal had apparently decided to make his main attack on the right flank of the French advance, while a portion of the troops were to act more directly by Ohain in support of Wellington. The guns had the greatest difficulty in traversing the narrow miry lane that led through Lasne up to the Paris wood. Blücher in person cheered on his soldiers exhausted with hunger and fatigue. "Lads, you won't let me break my word." The leading troops without firing a shot reached the cover of the wood about four o'clock. Half the corps of Bülow were still far in rear,

The Prussian Advance on Planchenoit, 4.30 p.m.

[1] Letter of Hervey. *19th Century Magazine*, 3/03.

but urged by the sound of the cannonade and the importunate messages from the English lines the Marshal decided to advance. The two infantry divisions debouched from the wood to the right and left of the Planchenoit road, covered by two cavalry regiments and three batteries. On the open rising ground in front were deployed two divisions of Lobau's corps with two brigades of cavalry—a force some 10,000 strong.[1] An attack of the French cavalry was repulsed, but a forward movement of the infantry led to a fierce combat and a temporary check. The remainder of Bülow's corps now came up, and with the great superiority of numbers Lobau was driven back slowly towards Planchenoit. At six o'clock the village was captured, while the bulk of the French corps on the heights north of the village were being heavily shelled by artillery. Seeing his line of retreat threatened, Napoleon at once called up the Young Guard. Its eight battalions charged forward, and in a short time cleared the village. His flank now being temporally secure, the Emperor was able to utilize the majority of his Guard Reserve for an attack on the English position.

Attack on La Haie Sainte, 6 p.m. The Emperor had now to wage battle with two opponents. Lobau and the Young Guard would probably suffice to contain Bülow, but the English defence had to be broken before further Prussian reinforcements arrived. Ney was told that he must capture La Haie Sainte at all costs. The assailants on the slope were reinforced by two fresh battalions and some engineers, and after a desperate hand to hand fight the farm buildings were

[1] One division of Lobau's corps was with Grouchy.

forced, and the key of the English position captured. The gallant defenders under Baring had fired away all their ammunition, and not more than forty of them succeeded in regaining the plateau. A battery was at once pushed forward close to the farm, and all the available infantry of D'Erlon lined the Ohain road. The centre of the British line had been forced, and was for the moment bare of defenders. Two battalions of the German Legion made a bold counter-attack, the Brunswick and Nassau reserves hurried to the spot, while Vivian's and Vandeleur's brigades galloped up in support from the extreme left. To stand firm to the last man was the only order given by the Duke. Had Napoleon promptly launched his Guards at Wellington's centre, victory might still have crowned the French eagles. But to Ney's request for more troops he returned the petulant answer, "Troops? Where am I to get them? Do you expect me to make them?" The state of affairs was in truth as critical for Napoleon as Wellington. The Young Guard had been driven back, Planchenoit was once more in hostile hands, and Prussian shells were ploughing the ground near La Belle Alliance. The attack of Bülow had to be checked, and the only reserves available were the battalions of the Old and Middle Guard.[1] The Emperor was still in the belief that he had only one Prussian corps to deal with, and that if Grouchy did not come to his aid, he at all events was holding in check the main army of Blücher.

H. 390

[1] The recently formed regiments—the 3rd and 4th Grenadiers and the 3rd and 4th Chasseurs—though a part of the Old Guard, were in common parlance called the Middle Guard.

Recapture of Planchenoit Leaving the French skirmishers clinging to the edge of the plateau, the Emperor rode to his Guard and formed eleven battalions in squares along the chaussée from La Belle Alliance to Rossomme. One battalion of the Old Guard was left at Le Caillou, while two others were ordered to recapture Planchenoit. The veterans, supported by the Young Guard, in one impetuous charge swept through the village, and drove the Prussians some hundreds of yards beyond it. At the same time Lobau, on the left, regained part of the lost ground. By a single blow the attack of Bülow was arrested, and the Emperor could turn his attention again to the Anglo-Allied force. It was past seven o'clock, but there were still two hours of daylight. To the eastward Durutte, in possession of La Haye and Papelotte, was pushing up the slope. On both sides of La Haie Sainte the remainder of D'Erlon's corps was vigorously disputing the ground with the English reinforced centre, while Hougoumont was in flames. On the extreme left Piré's lancers had passed beyond the Nivelles road. The Emperor, leaving two battalions at Planchenoit and three as a reserve in rear of them, marched at the head of the remaining [1] ten battalions towards the centre of the English lines.

H. 398

Approach of Zieten Meanwhile the 1st Prussian corps was slowly advancing towards the English left. Zieten, leaving Bierges at noon, only reached Ohain with his advanced guard at 6 p.m. Here one of the

---

[1] Assuming that the 4th Chasseurs had a second battalion, as the regiment suffered practically no loss at Ligny (Oman, *Hist. Review*, 1904).

Duke's aide-de-camps preferred a request for 3,000 men, which was not granted, and shortly after, under a mistaken idea that the English were already defeated, the Prussian corps began to move southward towards Planchenoit. This retrograde movement was, however, checked at the urgent solicitation of Müffling. The head of Zieten's column reached Smohain just as the Emperor and his Guard were descending towards La Haie Sainte.[1]

<small>Muff. Life, 248</small>

The infantry of Durutte fell back before the Prussian advance, and the situation was very serious. A sudden and desperate final attack on the British lines afforded the only solution possible. Leaving three battalions of the Old Guard on the plateau, the remaining seven battalions of the Middle Guard were pushed forward towards La Haie Sainte and given over to Ney, with the order to assault the right centre of the English line. One of the battalions was to be halted as a support. At the same time orderlies were sent along the main line of battle to announce the arrival of Marshal Grouchy, and directions were given to the artillery and all available troops of D'Erlon and Reille to second the movements of the Guard.

<small>Attack by the Guard</small>

The numbers and formation of the attacking force has always been a matter of dispute. It appears probable that the actual assault was made by [2] six battalions of the Middle Guard,

---

[1] The Prussian advanced guard, mistaking the Nassau troops for the enemy, opened a heavy fire on them from their infantry and two batteries of artillery (De Bas, 721; *Waterloo Letters*, 22). The advanced guard of Zieten that took part in the battle was 6,600 strong, and was engaged for somewhat less than two hours preceding the rout of the French army.

[2] Cf. Charras, Ropes, Houssaye and Rose.

or a force some 3,500 strong. The direction of the attack was somewhat unfortunate. Up the Brussels road, at a distance of some 400 yards, was the centre of the English line. Success had already been obtained at this point, and the approach to it was to a certain extent under cover. Ney, however, decided to take for his advance an oblique course, exposed to artillery fire, against the most strongly held portion of the English position. Each battalion was at first formed in a hollow mass, but the subsequent movement is not certain. Whether they were meant to attack in several columns in echelon or in one or two large columns is a matter of dispute. It seems clear, however, that, in the smoke-laden atmosphere of the valley, the formation after subjection to artillery fire assumed first the appearance of one large column, the rear portion of which subsequently fell off and formed a second distinct column. The leading column, supported on its right by the battalions of Donzelot, struggled towards the crest, and despite the grape and canister of the English batteries and the guns of Van Smissen, reached the plateau to the westward of Halkett's division. The Guards, lining the Ohain road, stood up and poured a volley into the dense mass. At the same time there was a heavy fire from the nearest squares of Halkett and the front of [1] Ditmer's brigade of Dutch-Belgians, as well as from the nearest batteries. There was an attempt made to deploy, but in the resultant wavering and confusion the English Guards

---

[1] This seems doubtful. It appears more probable that this brigade of Chassé's came up later. Cf. Chassé, De Bas and *Waterloo Letters*. See also Appendix xix and the regimental histories of the Guards and 52nd Regiments.

THE BATTLE OF WATERLOO

charged in line, and pursuers and pursued in a mingled mass of combatants rushed down the slope.

Looming through the smoke now appeared the second column of the Imperial Guard. The pursuit was arrested, and the soldiers of Maitland hurried back to the main position.

As the attacking column climbed the slope, it staggered under the heavy artillery fire and that of the reformed Guards in front, while suffering severely from the flanking fire of Adam's brigade and the Hanoverians emerging from the enclosures of Hougoumont. Colonel Colborne wheeled forward a four-deep line of the 52nd Regiment, and its deadly fire was followed by a charge which was supported by the remainder of the brigade. The column dissolved in confusion, and the victorious line advanced cheering towards the orchard of La Haie Sainte and the Charleroi road.

Retreat of the Guard "La garde recule!" The cry is shouted in dismay, and echoes from rank to rank. The unbroken columns of Reille hesitate and falter. There is no sign of Grouchy, and the Prussians—cavalry, artillery and foot—fall on the retreating battalions of Durutte, while Marcognet, Allix and Donzelot see behind them a plain covered with fugitives. The Duke's [1] signal is given, and 40,000 English and Hanoverians, Brunswickers and Belgians pour down the valley

---

[1] The order for the whole line to advance was apparently given at 8.15 p.m., a few minutes after the defeat of the second echelon of the Guards by Adam's brigade. The Duke then rode forward to the 52nd Regiment, and was present at its attack of the squares of the Old Guard on the Charleroi road. The simultaneous advance of the British line with the forward movement of Zieten led to the rout of the French army (H. 440).

in a torrent in the shadows of the twilight. The four battalions of the Guard retained as a reserve by Napoleon on the Charleroi road made a vain attempt to stand, but fired into by Adam's brigade, and charged by Vivian's cavalry, they were obliged to sullenly retreat over the plateau.

The Anglo-Allied infantry advanced over the battlefield in columns of battalions, while Vivian's brigade on the left and Vandeleur's brigade on the right, with little opposition, rode down all before them.

The Prussian Flank Attack At the hour of the assault of the Imperial Guard on the Duke's position, Planchenoit was held by the Young Guard and two battalions of the Old Guard; while Lobau was giving way before the determined attack of the cavalry and two divisions of Bülow's corps. The cavalry of Zieten, followed by the division of Steinmetz, debouching from Smohain in pursuit of Durutte, was now attacking in flank, while Vivian's brigade followed by Adam's division was closing up in rear. The darkening light added to the horrors and confusion of a disorderly rout as a mob of fugitives fled past La Belle Alliance towards Genappe.

Meanwhile a desperate conflict was taking place at Planchenoit. The troops of Bülow, which had been driven out of the village at the point of the bayonet, were reinforced at half-past seven o'clock by the two remaining divisions of his corps and the cavalry of Pirch's corps. The Prussian artillery had set many of the houses on fire when the assault took place. The ten battalions of the Guard afforded a stubborn resistance. The church and cemetery were the scene of a hand to hand fight, and it was only one by one that the houses fell into the hands of the assailants. The village was finally turned on both flanks, and the fugitives hotly pursued down the Genappe road.

The Rout   The great French army was now but a disorderly rabble in panic-stricken flight. The remnants of the Old Guard maintained, however, its high reputation. Three battalions in squares retreated in good order on the main road, repelling all cavalry attacks, while the Lancers and mounted Grenadiers slowly moved back more to the west on Genappe.

Wellington rode forward with the advanced troops along the high road to Genappe.[1] It is a matter of dispute as to where he met Blücher, whether at La Belle Alliance or at Genappe, but according to his own despatch of June 19 it was " on the road." The British army bivouacked on the field of battle, some of it as far south as Rossomme, and the pursuit was conducted with great vigour by the Prussian cavalry. From Mont St. Jean to Rossomme, from Hougoumont to Smohain and Planchenoit the ground was covered with the débris of a great battle, and with dead, dying, and

---

[1] " When the Duke called ' Halt ' that night, our most advanced troops were not within two miles of Genappe . . . on leaving Blücher the Duke rode at a walk to Waterloo . . ." (*Notes of a Staff Officer*, Basil Jackson [1903]). " About nine in the evening the two field-marshals met, when it was observed that without occasioning disorder the pursuit of the enemy could not be continued by both armies on the same road (Müffling's *History*, 37).

General Constant, who was riding with Wellington, states: " Nous cûmes de la peine à traverser le hameau de la Maison du Roi, à cause des pièces abandonnèes qui s'y trouvaient. Nous primes ensuite à droite dans les champs et comme il étail dix neures dans le soir, et nuit close, le duc ordonna aux troupes de faire halte . . . Nous revînmes alors avec le duc sur la chaussée, entre la ferme du Caillou et la Maison du Roi, et c'est la que nous rencontrâmes le feld-marécha Blücher, le génèral de Bulow et leur état-major " (De Bas, 758

wounded men and horses. The total loss of the Allied armies was about 21,000 men, while that of the French probably exceeded these numbers by 5,000 or 6,000 men.

The Pursuit The infantry and cavalry of the Imperial Guard sullenly retired in good order across the Dyle. The main French army was, however, hopelessly disorganized. Masses of fugitives, deaf to all orders, surrendered in crowds or hurried blindly to the bridge at Genappe. The long winding street of the village, blocked with wagons, was a defile impassable to numbers. The sabre and lance of the pursuing cavalry was wielded with merciless severity, and, escaping to the right and left, the scattered crowd forded the river and dispersed over the lanes and fields to the southward.

Blücher, with the infantry of the 4th Corps, halted at Genappe, while Gneisenau, with Roder's cavalry and but two infantry battalions, pushed on in the moonlight. At the sound of the Prussian trumpet or drum every French bivouac was cleared, and it was not till the early morning of June 19 that exhaustion put an end to pursuit.

THE COMBAT AT WAVRE

CHAPTER XVI

THE COMBAT AT WAVRE

The Attack by Vandamme—Arrival of Soult's Letter of 1 p.m.—Capture of Limale—Attack on Wavre—Combat of 18th at Rixensart—Grouchy Decides to Retreat.

Attack by Vandamme IN the afternoon of June 18 the right wing of the French army had meanwhile come in contact with the retiring 3rd Corps of Thielmann. At about 4 p.m. Soult's first letter (of 10 a.m.) from the battlefield arrived, and Grouchy, despatching Pajol with Teste's division to secure the river passage at Limale, galloped on to Wavre, where he found that Vandamme, without any preparation by artillery, had advanced the Habert division in columns of attack.

Thielmann with the 3rd Corps formed the rear-guard of the Prussian army, and had barricaded the bridges across the Dyle, now swollen by the rains. His rearmost division had crossed the river at Basse Wavre, and the main body was starting in its march from La Bavette on Couture when the French infantry appeared on the southern heights. A report was at once sent to Blücher, and preparations were rapidly made to hold the town and the left bank of the river. Two divisions (Kemphen and Luck) were posted on the high ground behind the town, one division (Stulpnagel) was sent to Bierges, while three battalions of the remaining division [1] and the cavalry occupied the river bank from above Wavre to Basse Wavre. The bridges at Limale and Limalette were held by three battalions and three squadrons of Zieten's corps, which had been left behind when he marched on Ohain.

The infantry of Habert gained the southern suburbs of Wavre, but their further advance was checked at the barricaded bridges, which were under fire from the loop-holed houses on the northern bank of the river. To go forward was impossible, while to retire subjected the troops to the devastating fire of the Prussian batteries.

Grouchy now pushed forward reinforcements, and endeavoured to turn the defence on both flanks. A battalion was sent to attack the bridge at Bierges, while Exelmans' dragoons were to endeavour to cross at Basse Wavre.

Arrival of Soult's Letter

It was about five o'clock when Soult's letter, despatched at 1 p.m. from the battlefield, reached the Marshal.

App. 15

[2] "At this moment the battle is raging on the road to Waterloo in front of the forest of Soignes. The centre of the enemy is at Mont St. Jean, so manœuvre to join our right. PS.—A letter that has just been intercepted states that General Bülow intends to attack our right flank. We think we can see a corps on the heights of St. Lambert, so do not lose a moment in drawing near and joining us so as to crush Bülow in the very act."

---

[1] By some misunderstanding the remainder of Borcke's division continued to march on Couture.

[2] A facsimile of this letter, of which the above words are the conclusion, is to be found in Houssaye.

Grouchy at once determined to leave the troops of Vandamme, now engaged at Wavre, to complete their task, while the remainder of his force was ordered to cross the river at Limale and open out the road to the main army. Pajol, meanwhile, with Teste's division, had picked up the cavalry of the 4th corps (Vallin) at La Baraque, and on finding the bridge not barricaded, charged across it with his hussars. The defending battalion was put in flight, and the passage secured by the infantry of Teste. The two rear divisions of Gérard's corps, either by losing their way or by some other unexplained cause, followed their first division to Wavre, and the whole corps did not get across the river till after night fell.

Capture of Limale

The Prussian detachment of Stengel retired slowly, keeping up a harassing fire on the advancing columns. Thielmann, realizing that his right flank was seriously threatened, moved his cavalry and all the troops he could spare towards the Rixensart wood. A vigorous attack was made in the darkness by Stulpnagel's infantry, but with little success, and all firing ceased about 11 p.m.

Meanwhile at Wavre Vandamme had made no less than thirteen attacks on the main bridges without success. Three attempts had been made to cross at Bierges, and it was not till near midnight that the exhausted combatants on opposite sides of the river ceased to fire.

Attack on Wavre

Orders had been received from Grouchy for the whole of the troops to follow him across the Dyle at Limale, but Vandamme contented himself with forwarding Exelmans' dragoons and the division of Hulot in the early morning.

The French bivouacked on the heights at Limale, covered on their left by cavalry. In front of them, from the wood of Rixensart to Bierges, was a comparatively weak force of the enemy. The corps of Thielmann was but 15,000 strong, and from these numbers must be deducted the detached forces of Ledebur and Stengel, who, for some unexplained reason, had marched to St. Lambert.

<small>H. 464</small>

Thielmann, however, knew that the main French army was in full retreat, while Grouchy had obtained no information as to the fate of Napoleon, and was apparently under the delusion that he had defeated the English. It naturally resulted that the Prussians at daybreak made an offensive movement against what was conceived to be a retiring French army. The advance of fourteen squadrons with two batteries had little effect against the formidable French force, which quickly assumed a formation for battle. Five of the Prussian guns were soon disabled, and Grouchy led forward his three leading divisions in columns of attack, flanked by the cavalry under Pajol. At 8 a.m. the Rixensart wood was cleared of its defenders, and a stubborn contest was taking place for the possession of Bierges. Thielmann now received a further and more definite report of the great victory won by the Allies, and heard that the 2nd Corps was marching to intercept Grouchy's retreat.

<small>Combat of 18th at Rixensart</small>

The favourable news put a new life into his troops, and vigorous and partially successful counter-attacks took place along the line. But at nine o'clock Bierges fell, and Pajol's cavalry had turned the Prussian right flank. Pressed at all points by a very superior force, a temporary retreat was necessary, and the 3rd Prussian Corps, covered by its cavalry, abandoned its position and slowly retired on the roads leading to Louvain.

The advanced guard of Vandamme had reached La Bavette, when Grouchy, at 10.30 a.m. on June 19, received the news of the defeat and rout of the French army.

There was no time to be lost, as there was every prospect that a part of Blücher's army would endeavour to surround and capture his force. A council of the generals was held, but it was evident that a retreat to France was inevitable, and Grouchy wisely determined to fall back on Namur. The march had to be commenced without delay, so as to avoid being harassed in rear by Thielmann, while a flank attack might be expected from some of the troops of the Prussian main army.

THE RETREAT OF GROUCHY

CHAPTER XVII

The Retreat of Grouchy

The Movements of Retreat—Pursuit by the Prussians—Attack by Cavalry—The French Rear-guard—Passage through Namur—Comments.

THE retreat commenced at about half-past eleven o'clock. Exelmans' dragoons (less one regiment left with Vandamme) marched with great rapidity on Namur to secure the bridges over the Sambre. The country roads were devious and in very bad condition owing to the heavy rains, but the cavalry advanced guard completed their march about 4 p.m. The 4th Corps of Gérard, preceded by its cavalry division, crossed the Dyle at Limale, and gaining the southern main road, passed through Gembloux and bivouacked at nightfall on the Nivelles-Namur chaussée near Temploux. Here Grouchy established his Head Quarters. Vandamme retired from La Bavette on Wavre, and, after halting for some time, subsequently moved on Gembloux, where his leading division arrived at 9 p.m. After a long rest the corps, at 1 a.m. on the 20th pushed through Argenton on Rhisnes, where Vandamme left his troops and rode on to Namur.

H. 479

The rear-guard, formed of Pajol's cavalry and Teste's division, kept Thielmann in check by following him up on the Louvain road. Then suddenly turning when Wavre was clear of the retiring 3rd French Corps, Pajol effected his own retreat by way of Sauvenières on Gembloux.

The whole of Grouchy's command on the night of June 19 was within a short march of Namur with a rear-guard at Gembloux, and the retirement had been carried out without any opposition from the enemy.

Pursuit by the Prussians While Blücher with his cavalry and his two army corps were pursuing the routed French army on the night of June 18, the 2nd Prussian Corps, which had not been engaged in the battle, was ordered to march on Namur and cut off from the Sambre the only intact portion of the French army. Pirch I, with his cavalry and three divisions, marched eastwards through Maransart and Bousval, and reached Mellery at 11 a.m. on the 19th. With a little more effort he might have gained Gembloux and intercepted Grouchy, but the Prussian troops, owing to defective Staff arrangements, had been under arms since the early morning of the previous day, and were thoroughly exhausted. A cavalry reconnaissance towards Mont St. Guibert in the afternoon detected that the French were in possession of the village, but no attempt was made to interfere with them. Thielmann, on the other hand, had been deceived by the skilful feint of Pajol's rear-guard, and did not realize that Grouchy was in full retreat till late in the evening of June 19. It was evident that if the French were to be caught up vigorous measures had to be taken on the following morning.

Attack by Cavalry

Thielmann started his cavalry—some thirty squadrons [1] with a mounted battery—at 5 a.m. in the direction of Namur, and the rapid march of these troops brought them in a somewhat exhausted condition in contact with Vandamme's corps near La Falise. At the same time—between 9 and 10 a.m.—the leading squadrons of the 2nd Prussian Corps were reported to be debouching from Mazy on the Nivelles-Namur chaussée. Meanwhile Pajol, with the division of Teste, had left Gembloux in the early morning, and marching by St. Denis reached Namur unmolested. The corps of Gérard, which was conveying the wounded and the artillery park, did not leave their bivouacs till after nine o'clock, and Vandamme had received the order to cover the retreat of the 4th Corps. The situation was one of difficulty and some danger. The 3rd French Corps, in the absence of its leader, had been surprised by the attack of Thielmann's cavalry and thrown into confusion, while some of the squadrons swept on southwards towards the Nivelles road.

French Rear-guard 20th June

Grouchy, who was at Temploux, covered the retirement of Gérard's corps by a strong rear-guard, and with Vallin's cavalry division galloped northwards and repulsed at all points the Prussian cavalry of Thielmann, who fell back on the advancing corps of Pirch. The 3rd Corps of Vandamme, resuming its march, took up a temporary position in the suburbs on Namur, and held the Prussians in check until the 4th Corps and the convoys had entered the city.

---

[1] The cavalry of the 3rd Corps had suffered severely at Wavre, and had been reinforced by nine squadrons from the main army.

Passage through Namur

The French army now passed through the town, and crossing the Sambre bridges marched up the Meuse valley towards Dinant, leaving Teste's division to cover the retreat. The friendly inhabitants of the city supplied a welcome aid in the form of rations, and lent boats for the transport of the badly wounded.

The Prussian troops had suffered severely in the attack on Vandamme's corps, and Teste, with great ability, held the ramparts of the city till darkness fell, when, with the aid of barricaded bridges and roads, he effected his retreat.

On the evening of June 21 the whole of Grouchy's command was assembled under the fortifications of Givet.

Comments

The energy and dexterity with which Grouchy extricated his force from a very dangerous position has been the subject of comment. At the hour at which he commenced his retreat from Wavre the troops of Pirch were at Mellery, but five miles distant from Gembloux on his most suitable and direct line of march. Pirch had been directed by orders from Head Quarters to combine with Thielmann in an attack on Grouchy. Every effort should have been made to keep up communication with the 3rd Corps and locate the French troops. A weak reconnaissance to Mont St. Guibert gained no information beyond that French cavalry were there, and it is evident that the 2nd Prussian Corps had no assurance that the French were retreating till the early morning of June 20.

At the time this information arrived there was no certainty of any support from Thielmann, and the fact may account for the slowness and timidity with which Pirch pushed forward his troops to the Namur chaussée on the morning of the 20th.

Thielmann, on the other hand, allowed the whole French force to march off unmolested before noon and gradually disappear from the Wavre battlefield, and it was not till late at night on June 19 that he became aware of Grouchy's retreat.

The combined forces of the two Prussian corps but little exceeded in numbers the troops of Grouchy, and to intercept him to advantage demanded concerted arrangements beyond the skill of the corps leaders. "The Prussian Staff, in fact, had been formed not only to meet the wants of the State but the demands of a mistaken professional feeling, and Grouchy reaped the full benefit of the error."

Chesney, 241

In connexion with the movements of the two opposing armies in the eastern area of the theatre of hostilities, the most striking fact is the little use made of cavalry as a reconnoitring force. Exelmans' loses touch with the 3rd Prussian Corps, and searches neither to the right or the left in his march on Wavre. Ledebur allows himself to be surrounded unknowingly by cavalry within a few minutes gallop of him, and Thielmann looks on in surprise when a whole French army corps appears before him at Wavre. Vandamme, on the march, allows hostile cavalry to unexpectedly charge him in flank, while Stengel, holding a bridge with infantry, is surprised that cavalry should unawares charge across it. "The eyes of an army are its cavalry" is a maxim that apparently did not hold good in 1815. The difference between light and heavy squadrons was a matter more of theory than practice, and horse and man were carefully preserved to ensure their efficiency in action on the battlefield.

The French nation had neither the desire nor the ability to continue hostilities, and the combined march of the Allied armies on Paris led to the flight of Napoleon and the restoration of the monarchy.

APPENDIX

I

Napoleon to Ney

Extract from Letter dated Charleroi, June 16 (about 8 a.m.)

"Je porte le maréchal Grouchy avec les 3e et 4e corps d'infanterie sur Sombref. Je porte ma garde à Fleurus et j'y serai de ma personne avant midi. J'y attaquerai l'ennemi si je le rencontre, et j'éclairerai la route jusqu' à Gembloux. Là, d'après ce qui se passera, je prendrai mon parti, peut-être à trois heures après midi, peut-être ce soir. Mon intention est que, immédiatement après que j'aurai pris mon parti, vous soyez prêt à marcher sur Bruxelles. Je vous appuierai avec la Garde, qui sera à Fleurus ou à Sombref, et je désirerais arriver à Bruxelles demain matin."

"J'ai adopté comme principe général pendant cette campagne, de diviser mon armée en deux ailes et une réserve. Votre aile sera composée des quatre divisions du 1er corps, des quatre divisions du 2e corps, de deux divisions de cavalerie légère, et de deux divisions du corps du Comte de Valmy. Cela ne doit pas être loin de 45 à 50 mille hommes."

"Le maréchal Grouchy aura à peu près la même force, et commandera l'aile droite. La Garde formera la réserve, et je me porterai sur l'une ou l'autre aile, selon les circonstances. Le major général donne les ordres les plus précis pour qu'il n'y ait aucune difficulté sur l'obéissance à vos ordres lorsque vous serez détaché; les commandants de corps devant prendre mes ordres directement quand je me trouve présent."

II

Soult to Ney

Extract from Order dated Charleroi, June 16 (about 7 a.m.)

"Monsieur le Maréchal, l'empereur ordonne que vous mettiez en marche les 2e et 1er corps d'armée, ainsi que le 3e corps de cavalerie, qui a été mis a votre disposition, pour les diriger sur l'intersection des chemins dits les Trois-Bras (route de Bruxelles), où vous leur ferez prendre position, et vous porterez en même temps des reconnaissances, aussi avant que possible, sur la route de Bruxelles et sur Nivelles, d'où probablement l'ennemi s'est retiré."

"S.M. désire que, s'il n'y a pas d'inconvenient, vous établissiez une division avec de la cavalerie à Genappe, et elle ordonne que vous portiez une autre division du côte de Marbais, pour couvrir l'espace entre Sombref, et les Trois-Bras."

"Le corps qui sera à Marbais aura aussi pour objet d'appuyer les mouvements de M. le Maréchal Grouchy sur Sombref, et de vous soutenir à la position des Trois-Bras, si cela devenait nécessaire."

III

Soult to Ney

Extract from Order dated Charleroi, June 16 (10 a.m.)

" Un officier de lanciers vient de dire a l'empereur que l'ennemi présentait des masses du côté des Quatre-Bras. Réunissez les corps des comtes Reille et d'Erlon, et celui du comte de Valmy, qui se met à l'instant en route pour vous rejoindre; avec ces forces, vous devrez battre et détruire tous les corps ennemis qui peuvent se présenter. Blücher était hier à Namur, et il n'est pas vraisemblable qu'il ait porté des troupes vers les Quatre-Bras; ainsi, vous n'avez affaire qu' à ce qui vient de Bruxelles."

IV

Soult to Ney

Extract of Order dated Fleurus, June 16 (2 p.m.)

" Monsieur le Maréchal, l'empereur me charge de vous prévenir que l'ennemi a réuni un corps de troupes entre Sombref et Bry, et qu' à deux heures et demie M. le maréchal Grouchy, avec les troisième et quatrième corps, l'attaquera; l'intention de Sa Majesté est que vous attaquiez aussi ce qui est devant vous, et qu'après l'avoir vigoureusement poussé, vous rabattiez sur nous pour concourir à envelopper le corps dont je viens de vous parler."

"Si ce corps était enfoncé, auparavant, alors Sa Majesté ferait manœuvrer dans votre direction pour hâter également vos opérations."

V

Soult to Ney

Extract of Order dated Fleurus, June 16 (3.15 p.m.)

"Monsieur le Maréchal, je vous ai écrit, il y a une heure, que l'empereur ferait attaquer l'ennemi à deux heures et demie dans la position qu'il a prise entre le village de Saint-Amand et de Bry : en ce moment l'engagement est très prononcé ; Sa Majesté me charge de vous dire que vous devez manœuvrer sur-le-champ de manière à envelopper la droite de l'ennemi et tomber à bras raccourcis sur ses derrières ; cette armée est perdue si vous agissez vigoureusement ; le sort de la France est entre vos mains. Ainsi n'hésitez pas un instant pour faire le mouvement que l'empereur vous ordonne, et dirigez vous sur les hauteurs de Bry et de Saint-Amand, pour concourir à une victoire peut-être décisive. L'ennemi est pris en flagrant délit au moment où il cherche à se réunir aux Anglais."

VI

Ney to Soult (*recently discovered Letter*)

Frasne, *Le* 16 *Juin*, 1815.
10 heure de soir.

"Monsieur le Maréchal, L'attaque que j'ai dirigée contre les Anglais dans la position des Quatre-Bras a surement été de la plus grande vigueur : un mal-entendu de la part du Comte d'Erlon m'a privé de l'espérance d'une belle victoire car au moment les 5e et 9e divisions du Général Reille avaient toute culbuté, le 1er corps a marché sur St. Amand pour appuyer la gauche de S.M. et ce qu'il y a de fatal, c'est que ce corps ayant rétrogardé ensuite pour me rejoindre, n'a pu ainsi être utile a personne. La division du Prince Jerome a donné avec une grande valeur ; S.A.R. a été légèrement blessée. Il n'y a donc en réellement d'engagé que trois divisions de infanterie et une

Brigade de Cuirassiers et la Cavalerie de General Piré. Le Cmte. de Valmy a fait une belle charge. Tout le monde a fait son devoir excepté le 1er corps. L'ennemi a perdu beaucoup de monde: nous avons pris du canon et un drapeau. Nous n'avons réellement perdu qu'environs deux mille hommes tués et quatre mille blessés.

"J'ai demandé les rapports des Generaux Comte Reille et d'Erlon et je les enverrai a votre Excellence.

"Agréez, Monsieur le Maréchal,
"l'assurance de ma haute consideration,
"Le Maréchal Pr. de la Moskowa,
"NEY."

"S.E. Le Major General."

The above letter has only recently been made public. The original is in the archives of the Ney family, and a photographic facsimile is to be found in Pollio's *Waterloo*, 226.

VII

NAPOLEON TO GROUCHY

Extract from Letter dated Charleroi, June 16 (about 8 a.m.)

"Mon intention est que, comme commandant l'aile droite, vous preniez le commandement du 3e corps que commande le général Vandamme, du 4e corps que commande le général Gérard, des corps de cavalerie que commandent les généraux Pajol, Milhaud, et Exelmans ; ce qui ne doit pas faire loin de 50,000 hommes. Rendez vous avec cette aile droite à Sombreffe. Faites partir en conséquence de suite, les corps des généraux Pajol, Milhaud, Exelmans, et Vandamme, et sans vous arrêter, continuez votre mouvement sur Sombreffe. Le 4e corps, qui est à Châtelet, reçoit directement l'ordre de se rendre à Sombreffe sans passer par Fleurus."

"Je serai entre dix et onze heures à Fleurus ; je me rendrai à Sombreffe, laissant ma Garde, infanterie et cavalerie à Fleurus ; je ne la conduirais à Sombreffe qu'en cas quelle fût nécessaire. Si l'ennemi est à Sombreffe, je veux l'attaquer ; je veux même l'attaquer à Gembloux et m'emparer aussi de celle position, mon intention étant, après avoir connu ces deux positions, de partir cette nuit, et d'opérer avec mon aile gauche, que commande le maréchal Ney, sur les Anglais."

VIII

Wellington to Blücher

Letter dated on the Heights behind Frasnes, June 16 (10.30 a.m.)

"Mon armée est située comme il suit. Le corps d'armée du Prince d'Orange a une division ici et à Quatre-Bras, et le reste à Nivelles.

"La réserve est en marche de Waterloo sur Genappe; où elle arrivera à midi. Le cavalerie Anglaise sera à la même heure à Nivelles.

"Le corps de Lord Hill est à Braine-le-Comte. Je ne vois pas beaucoup de l'ennemi en avant de nous, et j'attends les nouvelles de votre Altesse, et l'arrivée des troupes pour décider mes opérations pour la journée.

"Rien n'a paru du côté de Binch ni sur notre droite."

A photographic facsimile of the above is to be found in Ollech and Robinson.

IX

Soult to Ney

Extract from Letter dated Fleurus, June 17 (about 8 a.m.)

"L'empereur se rend au moulin de Bry où passe la grande route qui conduit de Namur aux Quatre-Bras; il n'est donc pas possible que l'armée anglaise puisse agir devant vous : si cela était, l'empereur marcherait directement sur elle par la route des Quatre-Bras, tandis que vous l'attaqueriez de front avec vos divisions qui, à présent, doivent être réunies, et cette armée serait dans un instant détruite."

"L'empereur a vu avec peine que vous n'ayez pas réuni hier les divisions, elles ont agi isolément, ainsi vous avez éprouvé des pertes."

"Si les corps des comtes d'Erlon et Reille avaient été ensemble, il ne réchappait pas un Anglais du corps qui venait vous attaquer. Si le comte d'Erlon avait executé le mouvement sur Saint-Amand que l'empereur a ordonné, l'armée prussienne était totalement détruite, et nous aurions fait peut-être 30,000 prisonniers."

X
Soult to Ney
Order dated Ligny, June 17 (12 noon)

"Monsieur le Maréchal, l'empereur vient de faire prendre position en avant de Marbais à un corps d'infanterie et à la garde impériale ; S.M. me charge de vous dire que son intention est que vous attaquiez les ennemis aux Quatre-Bras, pour les chasser de leur position, et que le corps qui est à Marbais secondera vos opérations. S.M. va se rendre à Marbais, et elle attend vos rapports avec impatience."

XI
Bertrand to Grouchy
Extract from Letter dated Ligny, June 17 (11.45 a.m.)

"Rendez-vous à Gembloux avec les corps de cavalerie des généraux Pajol et Exelmans, la cavalerie légère du 4e corps, la division Teste, et les 3e et 4e corps d'infanterie. Vous vous ferez éclairer dans la direction de Namur et de Maestricht, et vous poursuivrez l'ennemi. Éclairez sa marche, et instruisez-moi de ses mouvements, de manière que je puisse pénétrer ce qu'il veut faire."

"Il est important de pénétrer ce que veulent faire Blücher et Wellington et s'ils se proposent de reunir leurs armées pour couvrir Bruxelles et Liège, en tentant le sort d'une bataille."

In the temporary absence of Soult Napoleon dictated (probably on the heights of Bry) to Bertrand an order to Grouchy to send the cavalry division of Domon and the corps of Milhaud to Marbais and afterwards the above letter. The other readings of the text do not materially differ from the above, which is preserved in the Paris archives.

XII
Grouchy to Napoleon
Extract from Letter dated Gembloux, June 17 (10 p.m.)

"J'ai l'honneur de vous rendre compte que j'occupe Gembloux, et que ma cavalerie est à Sauvenières. L'ennemi fort d'environ trente mille hommes, continue son mouvement de retraite."

"Il parait d'après tous les rapports, qu'arrivés à Sauvenières, les Prussiens se sont divisés en deux colonnes : l'une a dû prendre la route de Wavre, en passant par Sart-à-Walhain ; l'autre colonne paraît s'être dirigée sur Perwès."

"On peut peut-être en inférer qu'une portion va joindre Wellington, et que le centre, qui est l'armée de Blücher, se retire sur Liège : une autre colonne avec de l'artillerie ayant fait son mouvement de retraite par Namur."

"D'après leur rapport, si la masse des Prussiens se retire sur Wavre, je la suivrai dans cette direction, afin qu'ils ne puissent pas gagner Bruxelles, et de les séparer de Wellington."

In the "Relation succincte" of Grouchy the last line of the above reads, "je les suivrai dans cette direction et les attaquerai dès que je les aurai joints."

XIII

Grouchy to Napoleon

Extract from Letter dated Walhain, June 18 (11 a.m.)

"Les 1er, 2e et 3e corps de Blücher marchent dans la direction de Bruxelles. Deux de ces corps ont passé à Sart-à-Walhain, ou à peu de distance, sur la droite ; ils ont défilé en trois colonnes, marchant à peu près de même hauteur."

"Un corps venant de Liège a effectué sa jonction avec ceux qui ont combattu à Fleurus. (Ci-joint une requisition qui le prouve.) Quelques-uns des Prussiens que j'ai devant moi se dirigent vers la plaine de la Chyse, située près de la route de Louvain, et à deux lieues et demie de cette ville."

"Ce soir, je vais être massé à Wavre, et me trouver ainsi entre Wellington, que je présume en retraite devant Votre Majesté, et l'armée prussienne."

Grouchy also wrote to the Emperor from Gembloux at 6 a.m., to the effect that his information confirmed the news that the Prussians were marching through Wavre on Brussels (H. 293).

XIV

Soult to Grouchy

Extract from Letter dated Le Caillou, June 18 (10 a.m.)

"L'empereur me charge de vous prévenir qu'en ce moment Sa Majesté va faire attaquer l'armée anglaise, qui a pris position à Waterloo, près de la forêt de Soignes. Ainsi, Sa Majesté désire que vous dirigiez vos mouvements sur Wavre, afin de vous rapprocher de nous, vous mettre en rapport d'opérations et lier les communications, poussant devant vous les corps de l'armée prussienne qui ont pris cette direction et qui auraient pu s'arrêter à Wavre, où vous devez arriver le plus tôt possible."

XV

Soult to Grouchy

Extract from Letter dated on Battlefield, June 18 (1 p.m.)

"Vous avez écrit, à l'émpereur ce matin à 6 a.m. heures, que vous marchiez sur Sart-à-Walhain. Donc votre projet était de vous porter à Corbais et à Wavre. Ce mouvement est conforme aux dispositions de Sa Majesté, qui vous ont été communiquées. Cependant, l'Empereur m'ordonne de vous dire que vous devez toujours manœuvrer dans notre direction, et chercher à vous rapprocher de l'armée afin que vous puissiez nous joindre avant qu'aucun corps puisse se mettre entre nous."

"En ce moment, la bataille est engagée sur la ligne de Waterloo en avant de la forêt de Soignes. Le centre de l'ennemi est à Mont-St.-Jean ; ainsi manœuvrez pour joindre notre droite.

"PS.—Une lettre qui vient d'être interceptée porte *que le général Bülow doit attaquer notre flanc droit*. Nous croyons apercevoir ce corps sur les hauteurs de *St. Lambert* ; ainsi, ne perdez pas un instant pour vous rapprocher de nous et nous joindre, et pour écraser Bülow, que vous prendrez en flagrant délit."

The above letter is sometimes misquoted. A photograph of the original is to be found in the last edition of Houssaye.

XVI

D'Erlon to Prince of Moscow

Extract from Letter dated Paris, 1829

" Vers 11 heures ou midi, M. le Maréchal Ney m'envoya l'ordre de faire prendre les armes à mon corps d'armée et de le diriger sur Frasnes et les Quatre-Bras où je recevrais des ordres ultérieurs. Mon armée se mit donc en mouvement immédiatement après avoir donné l'ordre au général qui commandait la tête de la colonne de faire diligence. Je pris l'avance pour voir ce qui se passait aux Quatre-Bras, où le corps d'armée du général Reille me paraissait engagé. Au delà de Frasnes, je m'arrêtai avec des généraux de la Garde, où je fus joint par le général Labédoyère, qui me fit voir une note au crayon, qu'il portait au maréchal Ney, et qui enjoignait à ce maréchal de diriger mon corps d'armée sur Ligny. Le général Labédoyère me prevint qu'il avait déjà donné l'ordre pour ce mouvement, en faisant changer de direction à ma colonne et m'indiqua où je pourrai la rejoindre. Je pris aussitôt cette route et envoyai au maréchal mon chef d'état major, le général Delcambre pour le prévenir de ma nouvelle destination. M. le maréchal Ney me le renvoya en me prescrivant impérativement de revenir sur les Quatre-Bras où il s'était fortement engagé, comptant sur la co-operation de mon corps d'armée. Je devais donc supposer qu'il y avait urgence, puisque le maréchal prenait sur lui de me rappeler, quoiqu'il eut reçu la note dont j'ai parlé plus haut."

" J'ordonnai, en consequence à la colonne de faire contremarche, mais malgré toute la diligence qu'on a pu mettre dans ce mouvement ma colonne n'a pu paraître en arrière des Quatre-Bras qu' à l'approche de la nuit."

" Le général Labédoyère avait-il mission pour faire changer la direction de ma colonne avant que d'avoir vu M. le maréchal ? Je ne le pense pas ; mais, dans tous les cas, cette seule circonstance a été cause de toutes les marches et contre marches qui ont paralysé mon corps d'armée pendant la journée du 16."

XVII

Chassé to Lord Hill

Extract from Letter dated Bourget, July 5, 1815

"Je me trouve donc dans la dure necessité d'exposer moi-même à V. Exc. le fait tel qu'il a eu lieu et la part que je crois que ma division a eue dans le succès du jour."

"Vers le soir, voyant que le feu de l'artillerie de droite ralentissait, je m'y portai pour en savoir la cause : je fus informé que les munitions y manquaient, je voyais très distinctement que la garde française faisait un mouvement vers ces pièces (Lloyd). Prévoyant les consequences, je fis avancer mon artillerie jusque sur la hauteur, et ordonnai de soutenir un feu des plus vifs ; en même temps, laissant la 2e brigade en reserve ; je formai la 1er brigade commandée par le colonel Detmers en colonnes serrés et chargeai la garde française.[1] J'eus le bonheur de la voir replier devand moi."

XVIII

Order of Battle of Anglo-Allied Army under F.M. the Duke of Wellington

First Corps. General the Prince of Orange.

1st Division (Major-General G. Cooke)
- 1st British Brigade (Major-General P. Maitland).
- 2nd British Brigade (Major-General Sir J. Byng).

3rd Division (Lieut.-General Count Alten)
- 5th British Brigade (Major-General Sir C. Halkett).
- 2nd K.G.L. Brigade (Colonel Baron von Ompteda).
- 1st Hanoverian Brigade (Major-General Count Kilmansegge).

---

[1] According to De Bas this was the second attacking column of the Guard. Colonel von Deelen, the Chief of the Staff of Chassé's division, states that three battalions of Detmer's brigade were ordered into front line by an English aide-de-camp (apparently to the left of Maitland's Guards), and that Chassé subsequently brought up the other three battalions. But the account of the movement is confused, and it is not clear how the two half-brigades became united in one column.

The repulse of the French Guard as represented on Sibborne's model is admitted to be imperfect, and the part played by the Belgians—however great or small it may be—has never been properly acknowledged.

APPENDIX

2nd Netherlands Division
(Lieut.-General Baron de Perponcher)
- 1st Brigade (Major-General Count de Bylandt).
- 2nd Brigade (Colonel von Goedecke).

3rd Netherlands Division
(Lieut.-General Baron Chassé)
- 1st Brigade (Colonel H. Detmers).
- 2nd Brigade (Major-General K. d'Aubremé).

Netherlands Cavalry Division
(Lieut.-General Baron de Collaert)
- Heavy Brigade (Major-General A. Trip).
- 1st Light Brigade (Major-General Baron de Ghigny).
- 2nd Light Brigade (Major-General Baron van Merlen).

SECOND CORPS. Lieut-General Lord Hill.

2nd Division
(Lieut.-General Sir H. Clinton)
- 3rd British Brigade (Major-General F. Adam).
- 1st K.G.L. Brigade (Colonel C. du Plat).
- 3rd Hanoverian Brigade (Colonel W. Halkett).

4th Division
(Lieut.-General Sir C. Colville)
- 4th British Brigade (Colonel H. Mitchell).
- 6th British Brigade (Major-General G. Johnstone).
- 6th Hanoverian Brigade (Major-General Sir J. Lyon).

1st Netherlands Division
(Lieut.-General J. Stedman)
- 1st Brigade (Major-General F. d'Hauw).
- 2nd Brigade (Major-General D. de Eerens).

Indian Brigade (Major-General G. Busman).

RESERVE. The Duke of Wellington.

5th Division
(Lieut.-General Sir T. Picton)
- 8th British Brigade (Major-General Sir J. Kempt).
- 9th British Brigade (Major-General Sir D. Pack).
- 5th Hanoverian Brigade (Colonel Vincke).

6th Division (Lieut.-General Sir L. Cole)
{ 10th British Brigade (Major-General Sir J. Lambert).
4th Hanoverian Brigade (Colonel Best).

7th Division
{ 7th British Brigade
Garrison Troops

Hanoverian Reserve Corps
(Lieut.-General Count von der Decken).
Brunswick Corps
(The Duke of Brunswick).
Nassau Contingent
(Major-General von Kruse).

CAVALRY CORPS. Lieut.-General Earl of Uxbridge.

1st Brigade . . . . . Major-General Lord E. Somerset.
2nd Brigade . . . . Major-General Sir W. Ponsonby.
3rd Brigade . . . . Major-General Sir W. von Dörnberg.
4th Brigade . . . . Major-General Sir J. Vandeleur.
5th Brigade . . . . Major-General Sir C. Grant.
6th Brigade . . . . Major-General Sir H. Vivian.
7th Brigade . . . . Colonel Baron Arenschildt.
Hanoverian Brigade . . Colonel Baron von Estorff.

Artillery under the command of Colonel Sir G. Wood.
Engineers under the command of Colonel Smyth.

XIX

DISTRIBUTION OF WELLINGTON'S ARMY AT 11 A.M. AT WATERLOO

In Front Line (including advanced posts)	4th Division (Colville)	Brigade of Mitchell . .	1,767
	1st Division (Cooke)	Brigades of Maitland and Byng	3,211
	3rd Division (Alten)	Brigades of Ompteda, Kilmansegge and Halkett	6,311
	5th Division (Picton)	Brigades of Pack, Kempt and Vincke	6,037
	6th Division (Cole)	Brigade of Best . .	2,582
	2nd D.B. Division (Perponcher)	Brigades of Bylandt and Saxe-Weimar	6,733
	Nassau Contingent	One Battalion .	900
	4th Cavalry Brigade (Vandeleur)	. . . .	1,075
	6th Cavalry Brigade (Vivian)	. . .	1,244
	Artillery .	4 Troops and 6 Foot Batteries	1,400

= 31,260

APPENDIX

In Second Line of Cavalry	5th Brigade (Grant)		1,162
	Cumberland Hussars		497
	3rd Brigade (Dörnberg)		1,268
	7th Brigade (Arenschildt)		622
	1st Brigade (Somerset)		1,226
	2nd Brigade (Ponsonby)		1,181
	Artillery	5 Troops	800
			= 6,756
Reserve in Rear of Right	2nd Division Clinton	Brigades of Adam, Duplat and Halkett	6,767
	Brunswick Corps		5,451
	Nassau Corps		1,980
	Artillery	2 Troops and 2 Foot Batteries	800
			= 14,998
Central Reserve	Dutch-Belgian Division of Cavalry		3,205
	6th Division (Cole)	Brigade of Lambert	2,128
	Artillery	2 Troops, 2 Foot Batteries and Ammunition Column	2,145
			= 7,478
Right Detachment	Chassé's Division		6,669
	Artillery	1 Troop, 1 Foot Battery	500
			= 7,169

GRAND TOTAL (from Sibborne) = 67,661 men.

N.B.—The total artillery force was 5,645 men, but the numbers in each line is only approximate. There were 14 Horse Artillery troops and 11 foot batteries, amounting altogether to 158 guns (De Bas, iii. 684). At about one o'clock there were 62 guns in front of the Ohain road to the west of the main chaussée, while 34 guns were in rear of the road as it ran eastward, but all the guns were eventually in action. De Bas gives the numbers as 68,841 (De Bas, 657). See note in Appendix XX. as to the numbers of the British troops being understated and those of the Allies overstated as regards the numbers of N.C. officers and men in the ranks.

XX

The Strength of the Armies

French Army   The numbers of the troops composing the French army are derived from states of different dates; and from the circumstance that men were in process of joining on the days preceding June 14, there are naturally slight discrepancies in different accounts.

Lettow-Vorbeck gives a total of 122,408 officers and men, while De Bas gives the figures for June 10 as 123,033.

The detailed states of the French corps are to be found in De Bas, and make it clear that the numbers given by Houssaye of 124,139 include the officers. Ropes, taking his figures from Charras, makes an obvious mistake in deducting the artillery park and pontoons as non-combatants.

Prussian Army   Lettow-Vorbeck adopts the same sources for his figures as De Bas, and makes the total number of combatants, including officers and bandsmen, as 123,073. Charras, by a modification of Wagner's figures, arrives at nearly the same result; but Ropes, in following him, makes a mistake in leaving out the artillery park. The organization of the "park-Kolonnen" was not in all cases complete, and some of them had not joined their corps on June 15.

Allied Army   An analysis of the Netherlands states given by De Bas makes it clear that the numbers of the Anglo-Allied field force has hitherto been understated. By a reference to the Waterloo state it will be seen that the figures for the British troops given by Sibborne, and generally accepted, are for the rank and file only of the British cavalry and infantry. They do not include the sergeants, trumpeters and drummers. But a comparison of Sibborne's numbers with those of the Netherlands states, show that to the rank and file of the British army he adds the officers, non-commissioned officers, and men of the Netherlands divisions and of the Netherlands cavalry.

De Bas in his calculations falls into the error of confusing the British "rank and file" with the "under officieren en minderen," the "manschappen," and the "troepen," of different states. I cannot reconcile the figures given by Sibborne for the King's German Legion with either the Waterloo state or the return of May 25, and he apparently underestimates the numbers by 619.

I estimate the strength as follows:—

British rank and file and N.C. officers and men of the Allied forces	92,972
British N.C. officers, drummers, and trumpeters in field force (from Waterloo state)	3,534
German Legion understated	619
Officers { British 2,087 / Allies 1,649 }	3,736
Total field force in officers and men	100,861

It is a matter of doubt as to whether the officers of the Hanoverian brigades and the Brunswick Corps are included or not in the above total. To get greater accuracy the original states would have to be compared, and the arithmetical errors in the Waterloo state corrected.

In the Record office are to be found the General States for May 25 and June 25 for the British, German Legion, and Hanoverian troops, as well as the regimental states and muster rolls for the same dates. De Bas has access to many hitherto unpublished data as to the Netherland forces, and with the lists of killed and wounded it ought to be possible to compute with accuracy the actual force that took part in the battle of June 18. There seems to be little doubt that the numbers given by Sibborne are incorrect, and require to be increased.

XXI

THE ATTACK OF ZIETEN AND ITS CONSEQUENCES

The casualty list is on the whole the best proof of the nature of a fight. From the time the first batteries of Zieten came into action till the French retired in disorder was something less than two hours. The total loss of the 1st Brigade—some 6,600 strong—was 8 officers and 200 men killed and wounded.

When the Prussian attack commenced Durutte withdrew his troops from Smohain and Frichermont to the heights behind the villages. Further to his left Marcognet had pushed forward by La Haye and Papelotte to the left of the English line. To engage Durutte, and at the same time link the attacking force with the Anglo-Allied position, necessitated a wide extension, which led to all the Prussian reserves being absorbed in a weak front line. The moral effect of the appearance of the Prussian troops in support of the Anglo-Allied left was undoubtedly great, but it is doubtful if the result of the battle would have been altered, even if they had not appeared. The main advantage gained by the Duke was that he was able to move Vivian's and Vandeleur's cavalry to the support of his threatened right flank, and even here their services were only required for the pursuit. After the great cavalry attack of Ney, the Emperor had concentrated all his efforts on the position between Hougoumont and La Haie Sainte. The attack more to the eastward was merely subsidiary, and even if carried out by the disheartened troops of Marcognet and Durutte, would have led to but a local success. The battle was decided on the right flank of the position, and it cannot be urged that the attack of the Guard was influenced even by the moral effect of the advance of troops of whose presence they were ignorant. "The fact that the enemy's Guard battalions remained masters of Planchenoit until Wellington was at last successful, snatched from the Prussians the laurels of the day. These would have fallen to them had they broken through and pushed forward to the farm of Belle Alliance, which the Marshal had assigned to them as an object. If Bülow had taken Planchenoit an hour earlier, he would have secured the decision on the flank and rear which Wellington was enabled to gain at the front."[1]

It must, of course, be remembered that the tactical success gained by the Anglo-Allied army was only rendered possible owing to the detachment of Lobau's command to meet the

[1] Das I Korps bei Belle Alliance. Pflugk Harttung, 239.

Prussian advance. The mutual confidence of Wellington and Blücher enabled each to act separately as to produce with their united armies at the right moment the greatest possible result. "Waterloo was, in fact, viewed in its proper aspect, but the crown and finish of a splendid piece of strategy.'[1]

"C'est Wellington qui a conçu le plan de la bataille de Waterloo. C'est sa resistance et l'intervention prévue de Blücher qui ont permis de la gagner. C'est la poursuite acharnée des Prussiens, après la victoire, qui a rendu la défaite de Napoléon irrémediable. La part de chacun est assez belle ainsi : il serait facheux qu'en Allemagne on ne sût pas s'en contenter" (Colonel Picquart).

[1] Chesney, 16.

PLAN OF THE BATTLE OF WATERLOO.

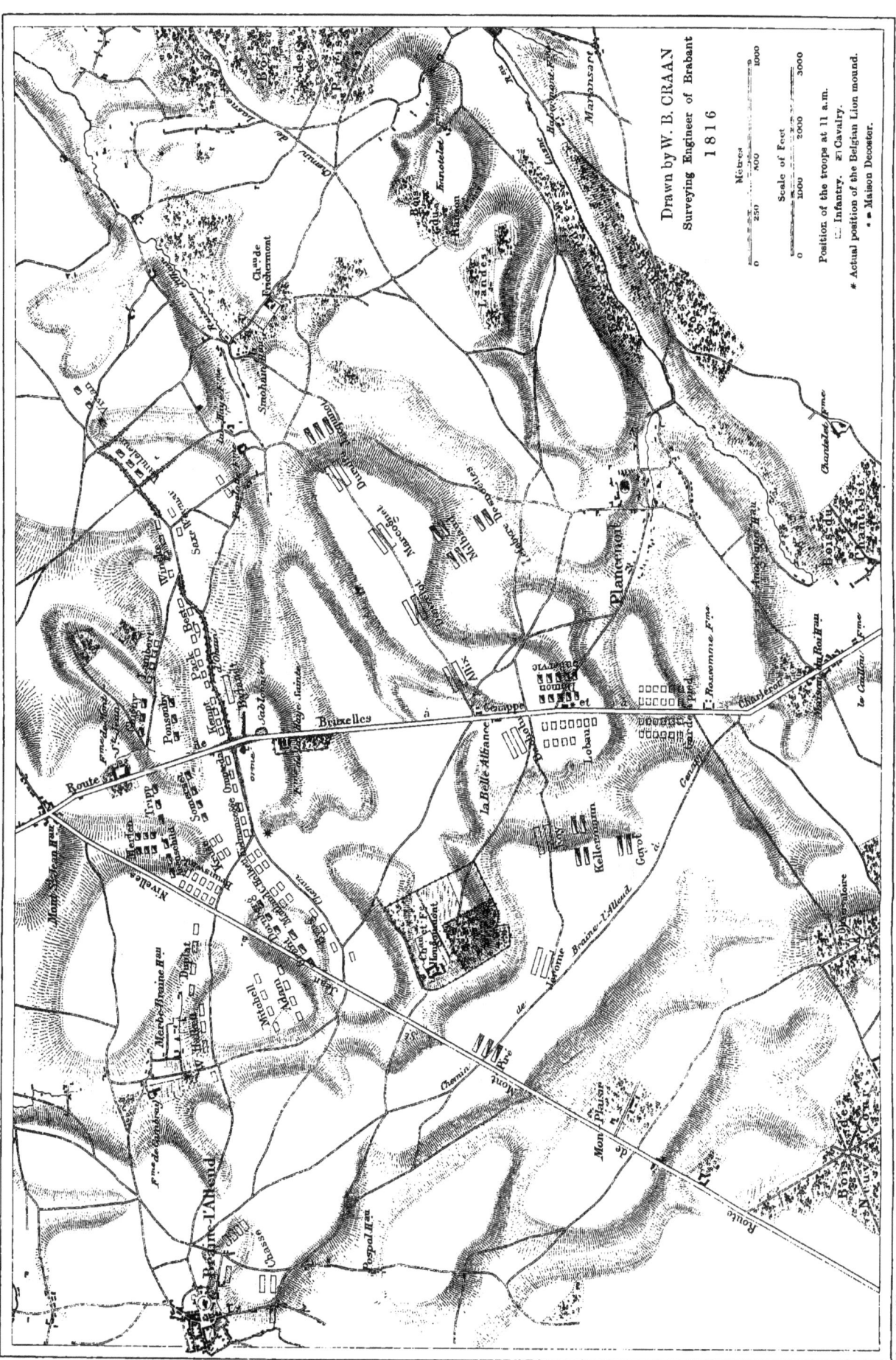

MAP OF THE MILITARY OPERATIONS FROM THE 15th TO 20th JUNE 1815.

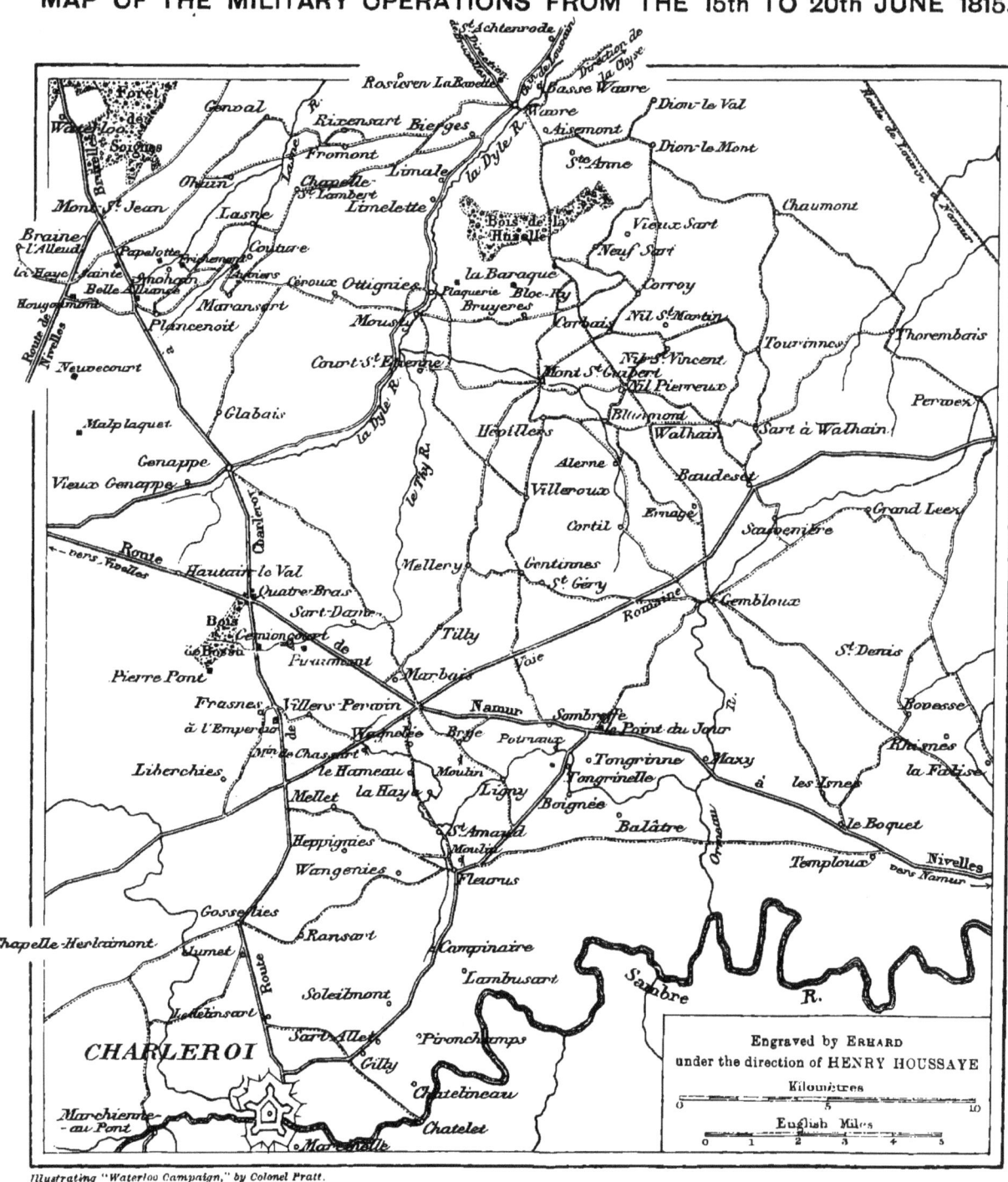

Illustrating "Waterloo Campaign," by Colonel Pratt.
By permission of M. Henry Houssaye.

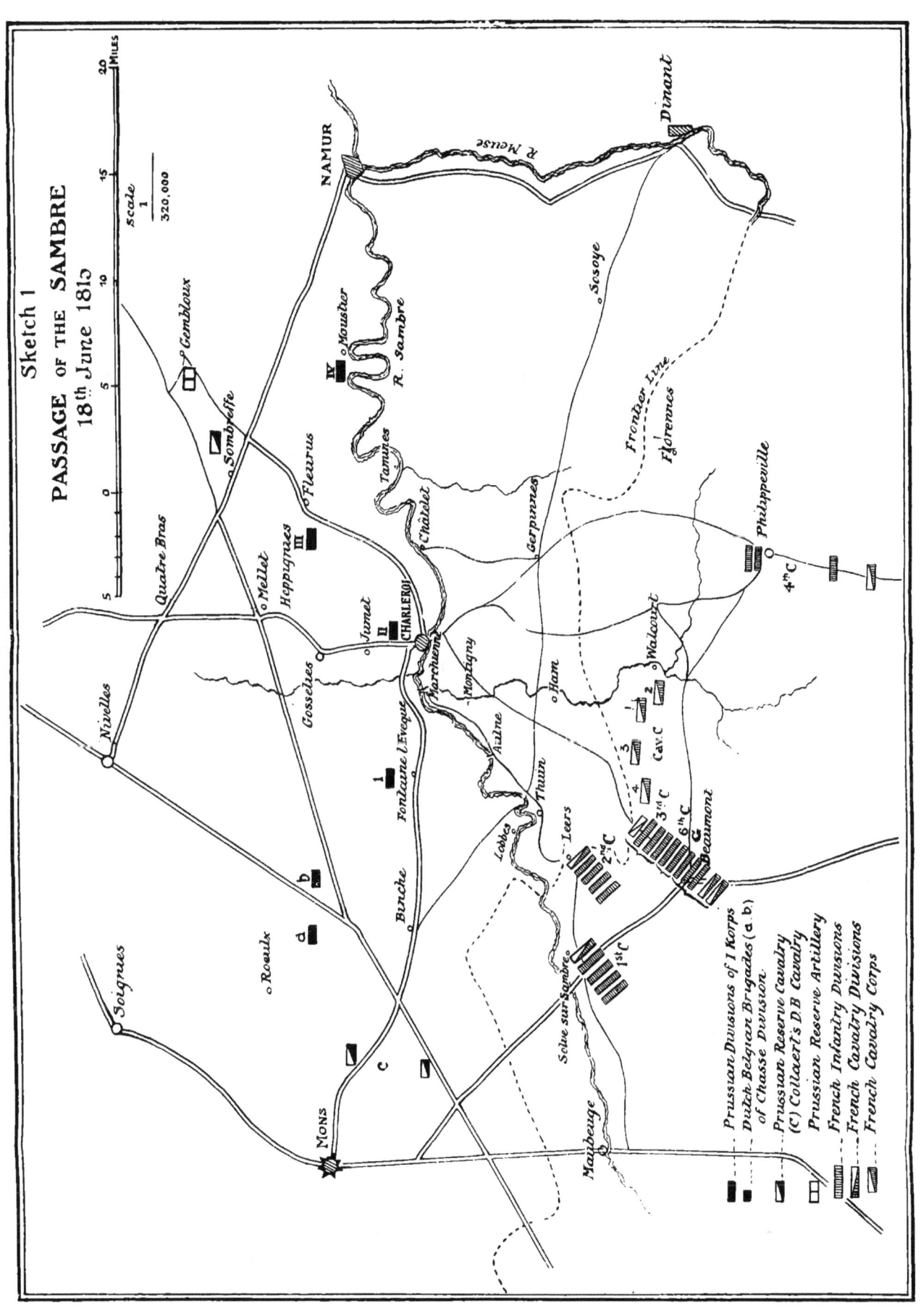

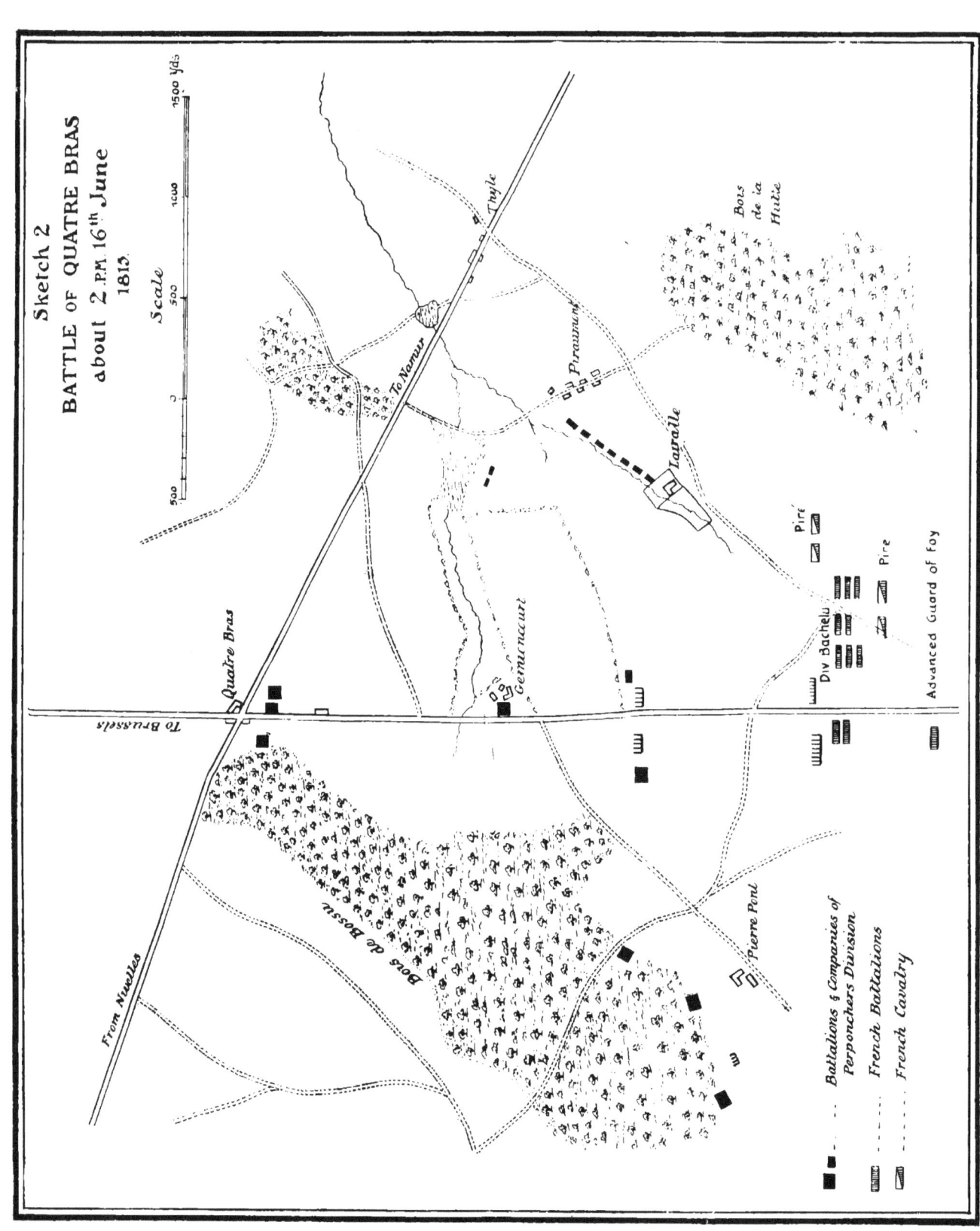

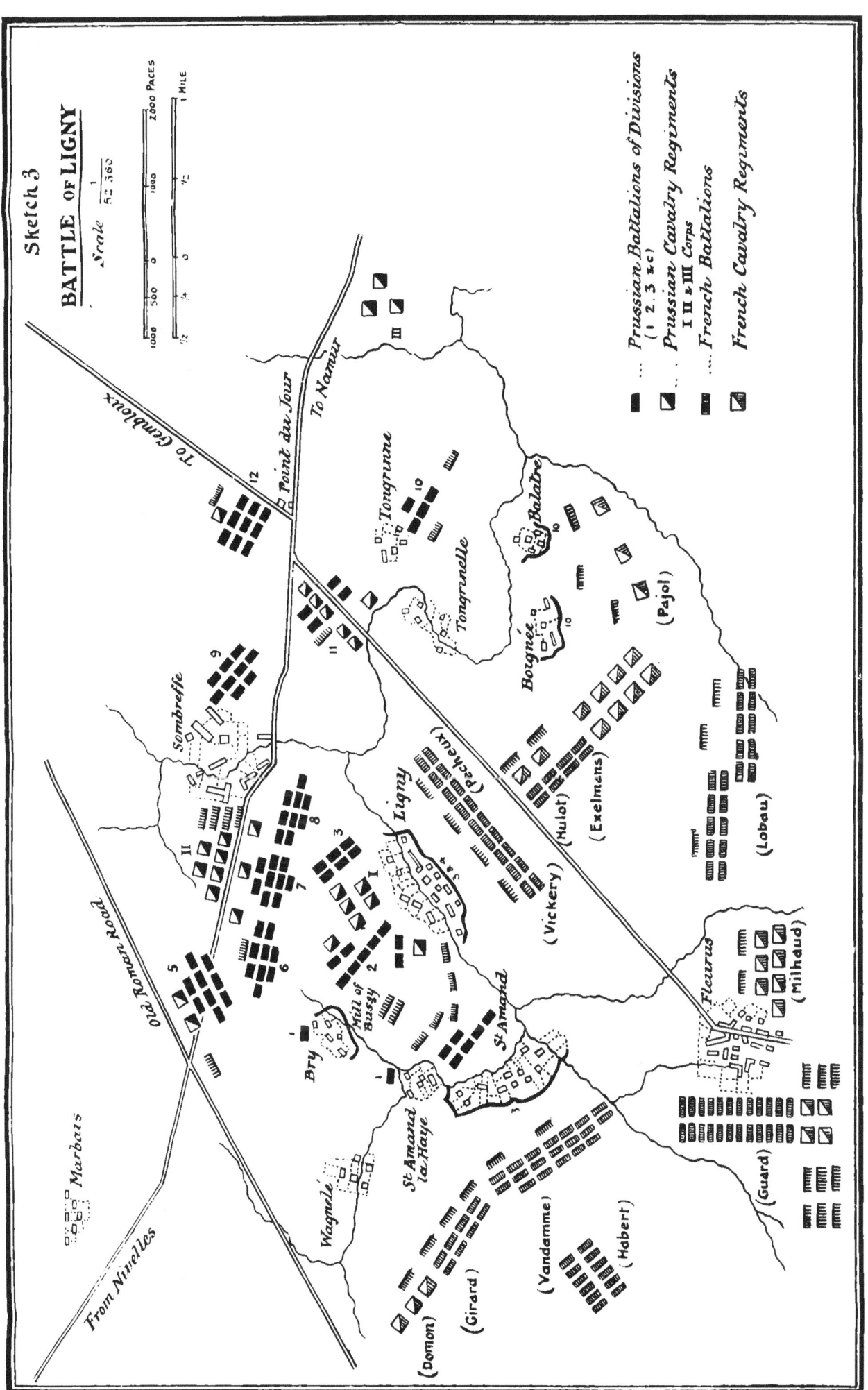

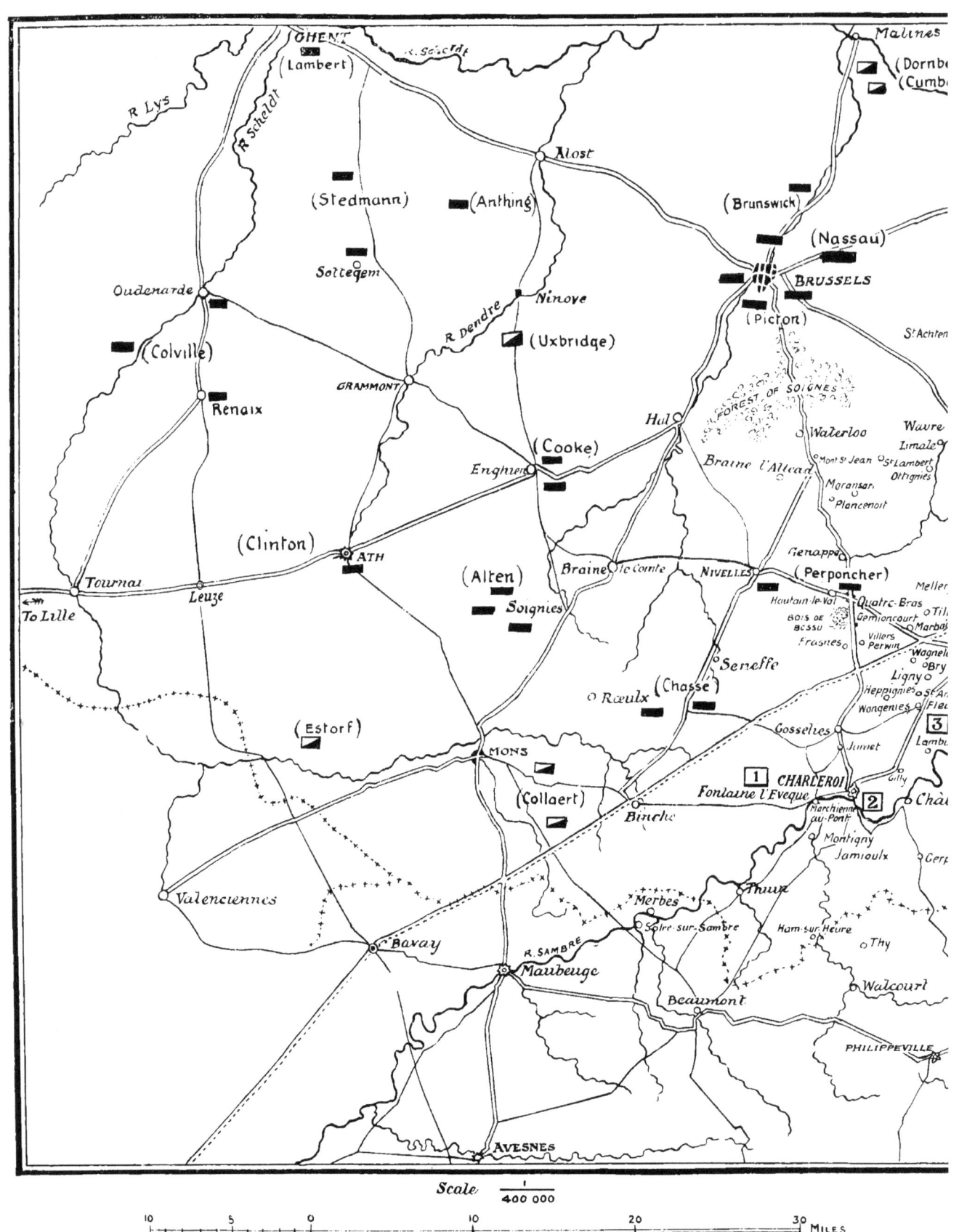

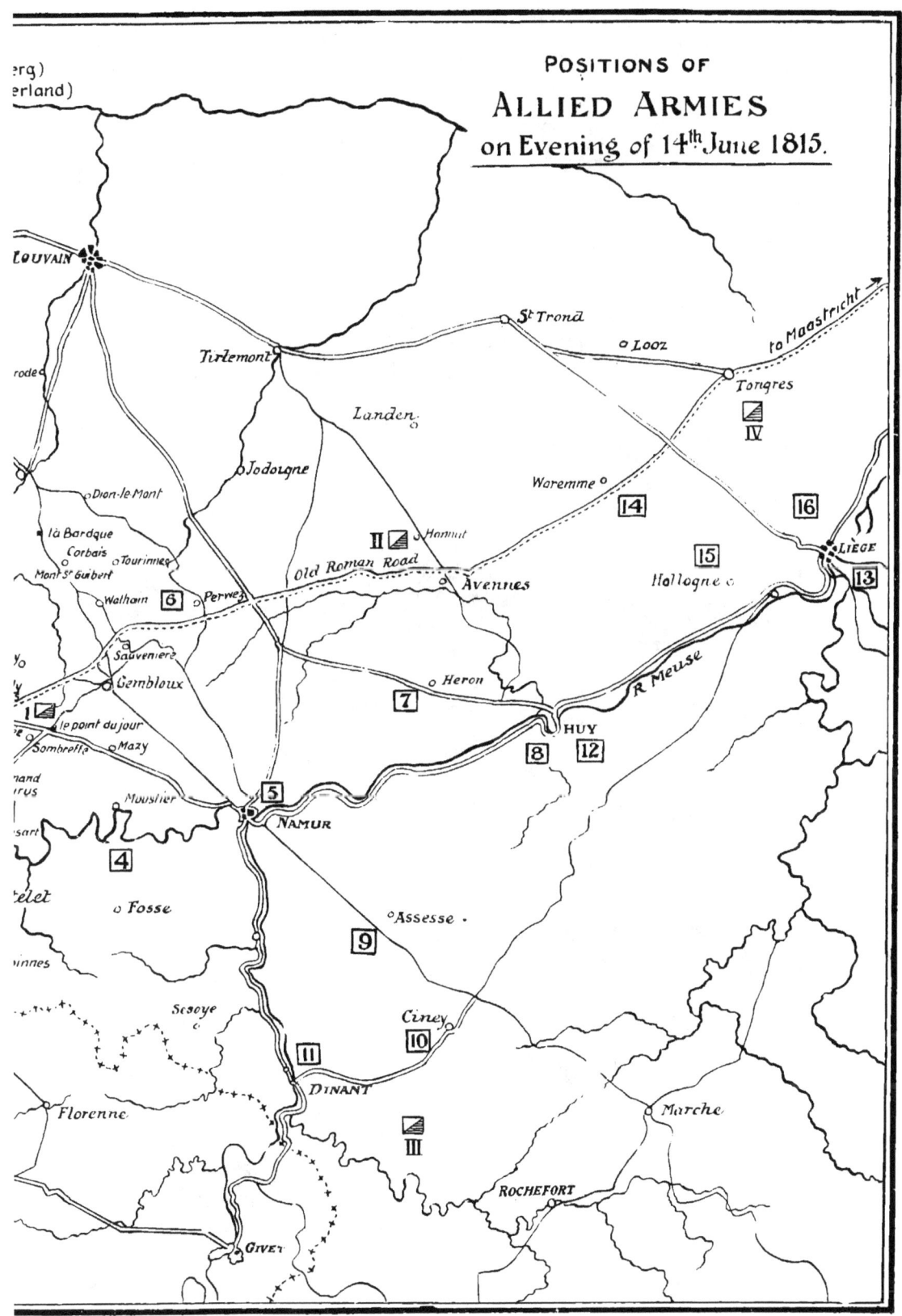

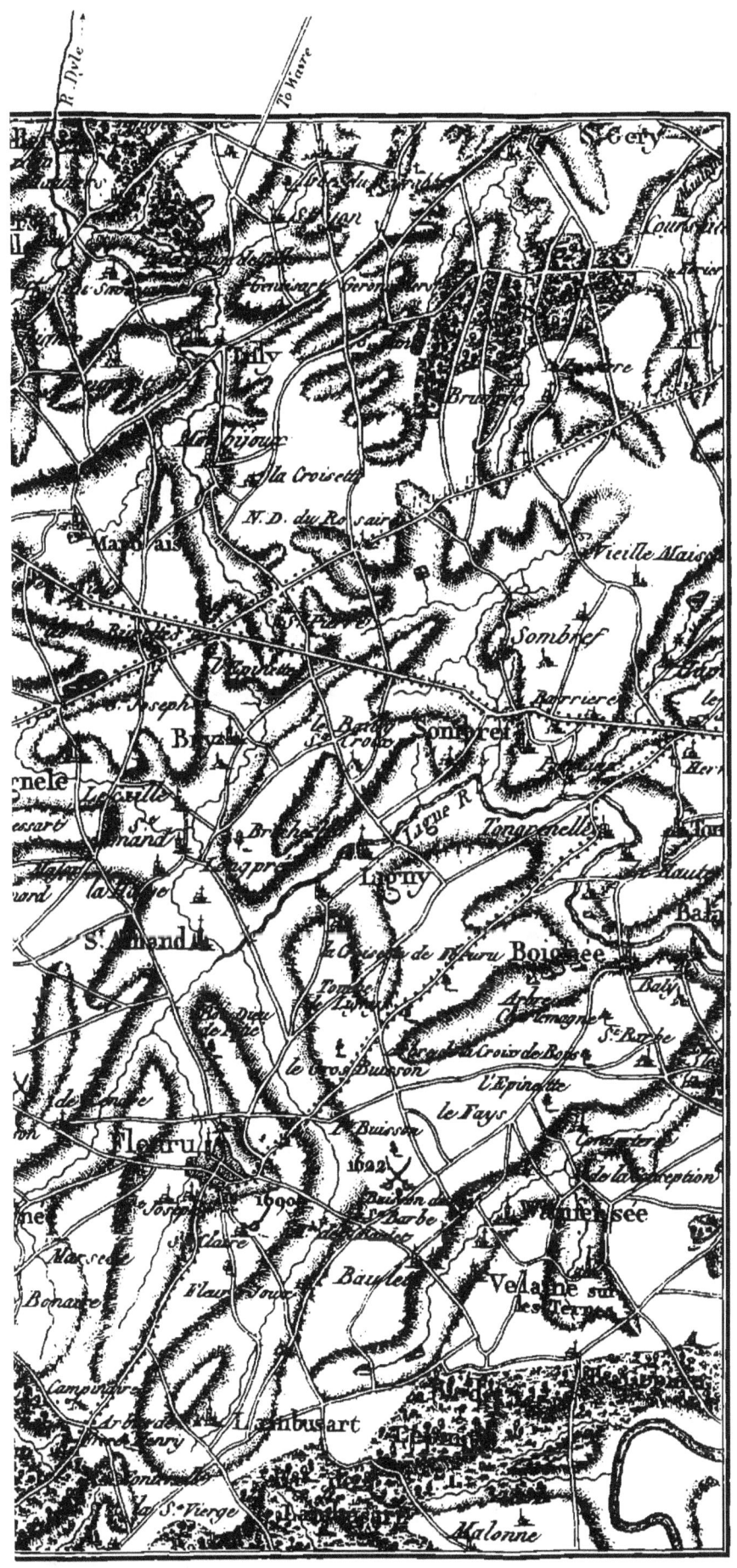